DESIRES
IN CONFLICT

JOE DALLAS

HARVEST HOUSE PUBLISHERS
EUGENE, OREGON

Cover by Koechel Peterson & Associates, Inc., Minneapolis, Minnesota

Every effort has been made to give proper credit for all stories, poems, and quotations. If for any reason proper credit has not been given, please notify the author or publisher and proper notation will be given on future printing.

DESIRES IN CONFLICT
Copyright © 1991 by Joe Dallas [revised 2003]
Published by Harvest House Publishers
Eugene, Oregon 97402
www.harvesthousepublishers.com

Library of Congress Cataloging-in-Publication Data
Dallas, Joe, 1954-
    Desires in conflict / Joe Dallas.
    Includes bibliographical references.
    ISBN 0-7369-1211-8
    1. Homosexuality—Religious aspects—Christianity. 2. Gays—Pastoral counseling of.
    I. Title.
    BR115.H6D35 1991
    261.8'35766—dc20   91-10270
                                                                         CIP

Printed in the United States of America.

16   17   18   19   / BP-MS /   16   15   14   13   12   11

For my beautiful Renee,
who never stops believing.

Contents

Introduction

A person can see where they've messed up in their life, and they can change the way they do things. So maybe my nature does draw me to you. That doesn't mean I have to go with it. I can say "yes" to some things and "no" to other things that are gonna ruin everything. I can do that. Otherwise, you know, what good is this life that God gave us?

—FROM THE ACADEMY AWARD-WINNING FILM *MOONSTRUCK*

During a quiet January evening in 1984, the conflict between my sexual and spiritual desires finally reached its peak. It had to be faced, and decisions had to be made.

I was 29 years old by then, feeling at least 50, and realizing that I had already lived three distinct and irreconcilable lives: a wildly promiscuous kid, a rigidly pious young minister, then a compromised adult who had tried—and failed—to mix Christianity with sexual sin, hoping against hope it would all work out.

The promiscuous kid was shaped by events that were mostly out of my control, at least in the beginning. I did not ask to be born sensitive, for example. But there I was: a shy, towheaded loner who felt every slight or insult a hundred times more deeply (or so it seemed) than other boys. I cried easily, which never helps a guy's social standing, and was awkward in groups. So I created a safe world of books, daydreams, bike riding, and long solitary walks.

Less safe was the real world I was avoiding: two older brothers who seemed light-years ahead of me in confidence, a highly driven dad who made it clear I wasn't exactly every father's dream son, and a strong belief that I was unacceptable, stupid, weak and, above all, very, very *different*. I have never pinpointed the source of that belief. I know neither my parents nor brothers really wanted me to think so little of myself. But by the time I reached my eighth birthday, I was certain the "reject" stamp on my forehead could be read from a 20-yard distance.

That was the year—1962, my eighth one—when my mother, having heard of pedophiles hanging around our downtown area, warned me to never go to certain theaters where these men were rumored to be. "There are men at those places who'll want you," she stressed. "So never, never go into that part of town alone."

Assuming that *wanted* meant "liked" or "cared for," I couldn't imagine what Mom's fears were about. So even as I promised never to go there, I began plotting how and when I would. Nothing sounded better to me than the thought of being wanted by a man.

That Saturday I rode my bike to the area I had promised to avoid. Mom had named a few downtown theaters that were considered dangerous. I located one of them—a legitimate but run-down movie house—stashed my bike, bought a ticket, and stepped into the lobby.

I lounged around there, munching candy and waiting for the movie to start, not sure what, if anything, was supposed to happen. Several other people were milling about as it got closer to show time, all looking pretty normal: couples, parents with kids, a few loners like myself. Not a sinister-looking character in the bunch. For all intents, the place was a typical theater showing a two-part matinee. Just as I was deciding Mom had worried about nothing, I noticed a middle-aged, friendly looking man striding toward me. Smiling.

What strikes me to this day is how normal it all seemed. I was standing by a movie poster when he approached. He asked if I had seen the film yet, what sort of movies I liked, and how many times a week my parents let me go to the theater. If he was sizing me up, I sure couldn't tell. All I knew was that a nice man was interested in me. In *me!* And I drank it up like a thirsty puppy.

I didn't want sex. I had no idea, in fact, sex existed, much less what it was like. But I'm sure, after 15 minutes of conversation with this genial guy who so obviously liked me, everything in my eyes and attitude was saying, "Whatever you want, as long as you keep liking me, I'm game."

He asked if I needed to use the bathroom before the movie started. I said yes, walked into the men's room, and found a stall.

He followed. Then he put a warning finger to his lips, looked over his shoulder, stepped inside, and locked the door.

When it was over, he told me two things that would impact my thinking for the next 21 years. "You're good at this," he said over and over. "You're really good." And he told me he had friends.

Molestation doesn't necessarily cause adult homosexuality, and many homosexuals have never been violated. But molestation does cause, in all cases, confusion. And confusion would become my theme as, over the next two years, I accepted money, gifts, and affection in exchange for sexual favors to this group of seven or eight men who had a virtual harem of kids at their disposal. It stopped when I grew older and less compliant, and I never told a soul until my teen years. But I had been awakened sexually and looked for outlets wherever I could find them. *Playboy* magazine became a primary source as I noticed my fantasies about the female body were growing as I reached puberty. A local liquor store kept the magazines in a rack easy enough to steal from. I developed a habit of snatching the porn, using it almost daily, and withdrawing even more into the dark magic of sexual fantasy.

When I entered junior high, I tried acting those fantasies out on any girl who seemed willing. There were a few, and we experimented to whatever lengths they would allow. So by the time I reached ninth grade, I had had many partners. By the time I reached high school, I had begun seeing adult men for sexual encounters as well.

The role of a promiscuous kid began its decline when an unusually beautiful brown-haired girl asked me during my junior year if I would like to attend a Bible study with her. Having no idea what a Bible study was, I accepted. I would have accepted if she had asked me to a dental visit. That's how enamored of her I was. She was kind, confident, gorgeous, and sexually unavailable—a fact she made clear from the start. But she seemed interested enough in me to ask if I would like to have dinner and then visit this new "church" in Orange County where, she promised, I would see "incredible things."

I couldn't have been more intrigued: a beautiful girl, dinner, and a Bible study topped off with "incredible things." The year was 1971, when the hippie movement was still in full swing and the country was ripped apart with social upheaval. It took a lot in those days to generate my interest. This date certainly qualified.

The church was Calvary Chapel and the speaker was Chuck Smith, who is regarded today as the father of the Jesus Movement and one of the world's finest Bible teachers. And that night, listening to Chuck's clear presentation of the gospel as being the only remedy for the human condition, a tug on my heart began. It would pursue me for three months until, exhausted from conviction and my resistance to God's grace, I found a quiet spot in a park across the street from my high school during my lunch hour, prayed, received Christ, and was born again.

Those were heady days—those wonderful times in the early part of the Jesus Movement. Kids were lining the streets in droves outside Calvary Chapel (and churches across the country, for that matter), waiting to find a seat, hear the Word, and grow. And grow we did. I sat under Chuck's teaching five nights a week, devouring Bible studies, loving my new life. The girl who had evangelized me knew her work was done, as I was in no position to pursue a relationship. Of course, I stopped all sexual activity and the use of porn. My life turned the proverbial 180 degrees, and I couldn't have been happier.

Then, a few months after my conversion, I noticed sexual feelings and temptations reemerging. I chalked it up to lack of prayer and spent even more time in private devotion, begging God to remove the fantasies and memories that kept intruding. And to my horror, prayer alone didn't do it. Fasting was the next step, then marathons of Bible study and more prayer. And still my eyes would wander over girls walking past me in the halls. My thoughts would go back to homosexual encounters that seemed a hundred years in the past. So I concluded there was something fundamentally wrong with me—so wrong, in fact, it made me one of the worst, most perverted Christians in the church. I had an unspeakable secret: I was a Christian who harbored very un-Christian sexual fantasies and attractions. And I was the only one.

That seemed obvious because no one—believe me, *no one!*—talked about having sexual struggles in those days. Which is remarkable, because many people spoke freely about their struggles with drugs, alcohol, or violent tendencies. We would routinely hear testimonials of people who had been delivered from satanic practices or life-dominating habits, and we would rejoice. We would hear prayer requests for people still wrestling with cravings for illegal substances, and we would sympathize. But no one, it seemed, ever struggled with sex.

I wasn't about to admit I was the exception. So I guarded my secret, even when I eventually entered the ministry full time, serving God and the church with a zeal that to this day amazes me. A new, independent church had formed in my city. When its young pastor invited me to join the leadership team, I eagerly accepted, leaving Calvary Chapel and becoming involved in the development of this new work.

Much of what drove me was love for Him. Much, I know now, was a fear of being exposed. I reasoned that the more I served God, the more I could atone for the wretched and (from my perspective) extraordinary sexual temptations I had on a daily basis. It never occurred to me that God didn't require me to rid myself of temptation; that my obedience was what He wanted and, in fact, was what He was getting. I never considered using pornography or bedding anyone outside of marriage. But that, I was sure, wasn't enough. I craved reaching a point where I'd no longer be sexually attracted to anyone. I would, I swore to myself, become completely clean and whole, absent of any lust. And a rigid combination of spiritual discipline and ongoing ministerial service would be my method.

For five years I tried. I preached, played the piano, taught Bible studies, performed marriages, baptized new converts, and conducted funerals. Sadly, the church I had aligned myself with became too big, too commercial. And as we grew in numbers and outreach (including regular television and radio broadcasts), we diminished in integrity. By the time I was 23, I had had enough and tendered my resignation.

Without the covering of the ministry to fall back on, I was especially vulnerable to the sexual temptations which had never really left me. And so began a decline I will go to my grave regretting. I started frequenting adult bookstores, picking up hookers, and eventually entered into an affair with a close friend's wife. It ended when she became pregnant and aborted our child. I began another relationship—this time with a man, the owner of a local gay bar. It lasted some months, then burned itself out. I realized I couldn't possibly keep this sort of life up. The bar scene, with its craziness and fast pace, was too much. If I was going to indulge myself sexually, I would have to find another way.

"Another way" presented itself when I heard about a church where you could be bisexual or gay, *and* Christian. This sounded better. I could engage with people sexually in whatever way seemed comfortable, yet still be a believer. Never mind what the Bible taught about sexual sin. I was way past concerning myself with the technicalities of Scripture. I wanted an environment which could pass as Christian, without any requirements—especially sexual ones—being made of me. The Metropolitan Community Church, often referred to as a "gay church," seemed made-to-order.

But I could tell myself for only so long that I had made the right choice. I could ignore what the Bible taught, give lip service to new interpretations that legitimized homosexuality, and refuse to see what looked back at me daily from the mirror: a man who was kidding himself. But every prodigal has to wake up someday. My appointment came in 1984. That January night I quietly considered, for no particular reason, where I had been and how long I thought I could continue the direction I had taken six years earlier. And that night, weeping but relieved, I confessed to God what He had known all along. I had been wrong, and I had to change.

This is a book written for men who have reached the same point: Christian men who are sexually attracted to other men but don't want to give in to those attractions. It's specifically limited to men because, although our issues often overlap, men and women's sexual issues are clearly different. I wanted to write a book about problems I'm familiar with—hence, a book for men. Female readers with a similar concern should turn to Anne Paulk's book *Restoring Sexual Identity*, also published by and available through Harvest House. Anne's work addresses lesbianism and related issues with an authority and experience I couldn't hope to match.

More than ever, people with authority and experience on this subject need to be heard because the problem of homosexuality among Christians is one of the church's best-kept secrets. Though most believers agree with the cliché "Christians aren't perfect; they're forgiven," there is often an additional (though unspoken) agreement that our imperfections go only so far. We admit we sin, but usually in "respectable" ways: an occasional lie, a touch of greed—nothing drastic. We seldom recognize sexual problems of any sort within our ranks. Rarely, if ever, do we consider how many of our women and men wrestle silently, but fiercely, with homosexual desires.

Yet the church is made of people from all backgrounds, who bring with them any number of spiritual, psychological, and sexual problems—homosexuality included. Our wish might be for such problems to vanish when people are born again. In reality, these problems often remain, challenging both church and defeated Christian. The struggling believer is challenged to resist his weakness through ongoing sanctification and discipline, while the church is challenged—no, mandated—to offer support and encouragement to the struggler. Both parties need to recognize the issues if they are to be effectively dealt with.

But who is talking about it? Amazingly, even in these early years of the twenty-first century, the conservative church seems reluctant to recognize it does indeed have members who are attracted to the same sex. It's a problem that's not supposed to exist within our walls, so those dealing with it struggle alone, silently waiting for deliverance and aching for the comfort of a listening ear or a bit of compassion. "The time has come," Peter warns in his epistle, "for judgment to begin at the house of God" (1 Peter 4:17). If we are ever to effectively address homosexuality in our culture, we had best begin by addressing it among ourselves.

Desires in Conflict was written with that goal in mind. It is intended to give reassurance and practical advice to the Christian man dealing with same-sex attractions, while offering insight to pastors, family members, and Christians in general. The original edition of this book was first released in 1991 and has been through subsequent reprintings since then. But in the summer of 2002, editors at Harvest House Publishing asked if I would consider updating it for a special rerelease. I was honored to comply and set about reviewing a book I hadn't glanced at in over a decade to see how I still felt about it and what needed updating.

Most of the original manuscript is untouched. One addition I've made is an Afterthoughts section, which I've tagged onto the end of each chapter. The Afterthoughts give me a chance to share some of my feelings and observations on each chapter in light of the years that have passed since it was written. I have also included an Appendix section containing articles relevant to *Desires in Conflict* as well. But the majority of the book is drawn, as it was in 1991, from the experiences of the men I have worked with as a Christian counselor. I drew largely from their stories when I first wrote this, and when I did I saw more than a few similarities to my own. Ideas for this book soon emerged.

The first had to do with process rather than transformation. Homosexuality doesn't just vanish when a person decides he no longer wants it. None of my counselees have been unclear on that point. As Bible-believing Christians, they no more wanted to be gay than they wanted a third eyeball. They were willing to do anything to be straight, but heterosexuality eluded them as a goal they could achieve through effort or faith. In all cases, the better approach has been one of growth or process—words that are becoming increasingly uncommon in our modern vocabulary.

We are people of the immediate, placing a huge premium on speed and convenience. We resent waiting. If it can't be had soon, we decide it isn't worth having.

When a person wants freedom from homosexuality, this impatient mentality can be lethal. It has led many a person to try shock treatment, exorcism, or sexual experimentation with the opposite sex in hope of a cure. The resulting failure and disillusionment is understandable.

That brings me to the second concept this book promotes: Homosexuality does not represent one isolated issue in the life of the struggler. Rather, it is symptomatic of other problems, deeply ingrained and often hard to detect. Like the red light on the dashboard, it indicates something under the hood needs to be checked.

Scripture bears this out. In the first chapter of Romans, Paul describes homosexual passion as a result of something else:

> Although they knew God, they did not glorify Him as God, nor were thankful, but…their foolish hearts were darkened….For this reason God gave them up to vile passions. For even their women exchanged the natural use for what is against nature. Likewise also the men, leaving the natural use of the woman, burned in their lust for one another (Romans 1:21,26,27).

Aside from condemning homosexuality in general, Paul is also pointing out its symptomatic nature. The problem cited here is universal sin, evidenced in rebellion against God's authority, of which homosexuality is one of many results. This holds true psychologically as well as theologically. The homosexual orientation is caused by several factors. In recovery, these factors—not just the orientation—need to be dealt with.

The third idea repeated throughout this book has to do with the complexity of the subject. Some of what we say about homosexuality is simple, biblically based, and easily grasped. We can say, for example, that homosexuality in all forms is unnatural and immoral, contrary to God's design. On those points we can be adamant. Beyond that, most generalizations we make on the matter will prove faulty. There is no such thing as a "typical" homosexual. There is no one reason people become homosexual. And there is no one method of dealing with homosexuality which will be effective for all men. An intelligent discussion of the subject should include a respect for its complexity.

So let me emphasize from the outset that I know of no universal "cure." Nobody does. Instead, I have taken the experiences of men I've worked with and have, hopefully, gleaned some ideas from their journeys that will be helpful to you in your own.

I have tried to position the struggle against homosexual desires as a part of the broader sanctification process all Christians go through. All Christians, of course, don't wrestle with homosexuality, but they wrestle with *something*. That's part of our common human experience. So chapters 1 through 4 place emphasis on obedience and integrity—the elements all of us need to have in place if we're to become more Christlike.

Chapters 5 and 6 are the most theoretical in the book. When borrowing from others' ideas, I have been careful to give full credit; when presenting my own, I've been, I hope, equally clear. Opinions are useful, of course. But just as the Bereans in the book of Acts searched the Scriptures to see if what they were hearing rang true, so you need to check the ideas presented in *Desires in Conflict* in the light of the Bible to determine how authentic and helpful a book it is.

While recognizing that no one can provide all the answers needed for someone struggling with attractions to the same sex, I do think it's useful to know what has worked for other people. So in chapters 7 and 8 I have mentioned specific challenges other men have faced, and am grateful for their permission to include them in this book. Not all readers will relate to all the issues raised and the suggestions made in these chapters, but I believe many, if not most of them, will strike a familiar chord in you.

I am indebted to Harvest House Publishers for their interest in this revised version; to my old friend Bill Jensen, formerly of Harvest House, who first pushed me to write this; and to the many respected leaders in the body of Christ who have promoted this book over the years and have thus opened countless doors for me. Dr. James Dobson, Dr. Jerry

Falwell, Hank Hanegraaff, Stephen Arterburn, Janet Parshall, Dr. John Ankerberg, Warren Duffy, Cal Thomas, Rich Buhler, Tim LaHaye, Beverly LaHaye, and Marlin Maddoux have all been generous with their encouragement and exposure.

Special thanks to the men who, through seminars and counseling, have allowed me to be a part of their process. They have once and forever changed my life.

One
You Are Here

*Then said Evangelist, "If this be
thy condition, why standest thou still?" He
answered, "Because I know not where to go."*

—*Pilgrim's Progress*

Your first trip to a new shopping mall will probably
include a stop at the main directory. It's centrally displayed
on each floor, giving an overview of the complex, with each
business location named and categorized. Visual creatures
that we are, we like overviews because they simplify things,
framing them with boundaries and definitions. So you appreciate the directory. It makes the mall less intimidating, more
accessible. The directory's reference point is, of course, the
spot marked X saying "You Are Here." It positions you immediately. It also marks the location of your goal in relation to
your current position, while giving a clue as to how long it
will take you to get there. And it lends some friendly support
to a bewildered shopper. *(See? You're not lost. Here's where you
are and that's where you're headed.)*

As a Christian struggling against homosexuality, you could
probably use a bit of that. Chances are, you've been applying

Herculean effort to the struggle, reaping a mixture of success and setbacks. Your best intentions seem to be no match for your same-sex attractions, and when you begin addressing all the conflicts that go along with homosexuality, you open more of a Pandora's box than you ever reckoned on.

The resulting confusion is understandable. After all, if your only opponent were a single issue (lust, temper, etc.) the fight would be simpler. But this battle is waged against a unique combination of desires in conflict: the desire to love God obediently versus the desire to be loved in a way that God prohibits, the desire for a normal sex life versus the desire to satisfy feelings that seem normal but aren't, the desire to be honest about your feelings versus the desire to be safe from embarrassment. It's not just a sexual sin you're fighting, but a deeply ingrained way of responding which seems immune to good intentions. In fact, you may be finding that the more effort you apply to the fight, the harder it is to believe you will ever win. "The good that I will to do, I do not do," laments the apostle Paul, "but the evil I will not to do, that I practice" (Romans 7:19). Sound familiar?

Effort is commendable, but without strategy it's futile. Good help in developing such strategy, though, is scarce. That's because in spite of the volumes written about homosexuality, not to mention the controversies now raging over its political and social impact, little guidance has been offered to people in your position. There have been some fine books written for the homosexual wanting to change, but they are sparse and relatively unknown to the general market, eclipsed by the more popular and ever-simplistic "If you're gay, accept it" versus the "If you're gay, you're damned" materials, both of which exclude you. You don't accept "gay" as a desirable state, but you also don't need to be told that homosexual acts are abnormal or biblically condemned. Hearing that is about as useful to you as a sign on the shopping mall directory saying "You Are Lost."

With so few resources available, it's no wonder you feel aimless or defeated. A sense of bearing is called for—an understanding of where you are in relation to your goal, what it is you're dealing with, and what you can expect along the way.

You—and Others!—Are Here

Lost shoppers feel isolated in their confusion. They assume the people strolling past them know just where they're going and how to get there. This only increases their frustration, making them feel all the more alone. So, of course, they're relieved when they come across another shopper at the directory looking as lost as they are. At least they're not the only ones!

When counseling men struggling with homosexuality, I'm reminded of a sharper, more consequential form of social isolation. It's one thing to struggle, but another to feel you're the only one struggling. Worse yet is the fear that if your problem were found out, the grace shown to people with "normal" problems wouldn't be extended to you. Time and again counselees report fear of exposure as their worst nightmare. Many of them are not sexually active and are committing no moral sin; they just know they are attracted to their own sex. Yet the possibility someone else might detect those attractions frightens them into silence and often avoidance of close relationships. Close relationships, after all, include the sharing of personal problems, and here's one problem no one seems anxious to discuss.

Time and again, when these men find a support group or therapist and begin to open up a bit, they're relieved to learn they're not alone. Or "freakish." Or whatever. It feels good knowing you're not the only one with a problem—not because you necessarily want other people to have problems like yours, but because you want to feel that somebody else understands.

We'll begin then by addressing the isolation experienced by other people in your position. The "You Are Here" in this case should be subtitled "It's Crowded Here." After all, since the Christian church is made of people from all parts of society, you can expect its members to represent a variety of problems. So with today's large divorce rate, for example, one would expect many divorcées and single parents to be part of the church body. Likewise, alcoholism and drug addiction are commonplace, so the church includes many believers grappling with the effects of substance abuse.

Considering the fact homosexuality is evident in all aspects of American life, we shouldn't be surprised at the number of Christians who deal with it as well. What *is* surprising is the lack of assistance available to such Christians, in spite of the growth experienced by the few ministries that do offer help.

Lack of adequate information within the church is often the culprit, and I believe this lack of information exists because we have been threatened by any understanding of homosexuality beyond a few select Bible verses.

Of course, the Christian develops his worldview and understanding of humanity from the Bible. That's as it must be. Scripture provides the standard by which we test all theory and on which we base our belief system. Sometimes, though, our understanding of an issue is limited because of our unwillingness to consider information not spelled out in the Bible, but which is by no means unbiblical.

Inadequate information among Christians about homosexuality is a case in point. While there are clear biblical injunctions against homosexual *acts*, there is scant reference in the Bible to the *homosexual orientation*—i.e., sexual *attraction* to members of one's own sex as opposed to sexual *activ-*

ity with the same sex. Psychological studies provide some understanding of the homosexual orientation, but many of us are understandably leery of all things psychological. (Considering the anti-Christian bias of so many mental health practitioners, psychology's ready acceptance among Christians is sometimes astounding!) Nonetheless, ignorance of research that *is* valid has left many Christians unaware of the complexities of homosexuality in particular, and human sexuality in general.

Most Christians, for example, view a homosexual only as a person who commits homosexual acts. The question of orientation is rarely considered. And so the notion of a Christian having homosexual desires is foreign to many in the church—particularly to those who are solidly heterosexual. It's usually viewed as a problem "out there" which no true believer could have. But true believers—more than we would care to recognize—*do* have it. Considering the Christian community's lack of understanding, who is going to be brave enough to identify himself as someone having a conflict, when that conflict is not supposed to exist among Christians?

Or, to frame it differently, when is the last time you heard a person in a prayer meeting request prayer for his homosexual temptations?

Lack of adequate information doesn't account for all the silence on the struggler's part, but it accounts for much of it. This leaves thousands of Christians sitting in our pews, having the same conflicts, bearing the same weight of secrecy, yet certain they're alone in their difficulty.

But the fact remains, you *do* have brothers and sisters with struggles similar to yours. While it is true that you and your circumstances are unique in many ways, it's also true that your position is not rare. You are here, but you are far from alone.

You Are Making Decisions Here

When you confront your status as a Christian with homosexual tendencies, you have to also confront your options: both the right and the wrong ones. No one is forcing you to change. You don't have to go straight, nor do you have to deny your sexual longings. You have choices, and making a clear analysis of those choices now will prevent indecision once you have started your course, because it's going to be difficult for you no matter which course you choose.

Don't misunderstand: I endorse only one choice—full repentance of all homosexual activity and an earnest seeking for sexual wholeness—because that is the only choice that has scriptural backing. It's also the only alternative which will be explored and commended in this book. But if you make this choice without recognizing the others, experience has shown you will eventually be challenged to determine whether or not your choice was the right one. If you have not considered the other options, weighed them, and consciously rejected them, you may be setting yourself up for wavering somewhere down the line. So you may as well settle it now. Recognizing the alternatives to a plan of action doesn't weaken your commitment to that plan, but it does settle in your mind what you have decided to do, what you have decided *not* to do, and why.

"How long will you falter between two opinions?" Elijah demanded. "If the LORD is God, follow Him; but if Baal, follow him" (1 Kings 18:21). The prophet was appealing not only to people's spiritual commitment, but also to their common sense. He logically assumed that before deciding whether to serve God or Baal, they would consider the merits of both. We will consider your other options in that same spirit.

Your choice is to repent of all homosexual activity and seek sexual wholeness, or you can decide on one of three other courses of action:

1. Maintain the status quo

2. Abandon the faith

3. Compromise scriptural standards

Maintaining the Status Quo

To be undecided is to decide. The decision *not* to make a decision is a decision in itself. Inaction, then, or maintaining the status quo, is a plan of action.

When questioning a counselee about his current situation, I'm interested in knowing what impact homosexuality is having on his life, and how it is being expressed. Are his sexual attractions predominantly homosexual? Are his attractions expressed inwardly (sexual dreams and fantasies), or is he acting them out with other people? If he is sexually active, is his activity limited to anonymous encounters, long-term relationships, or brief affairs? Questions of this type help define the status quo and the consequences of ignoring it.

If your struggle is strictly inward, limited to attractions, fantasies, and the like, you may opt to do nothing about it and find life bearable, if not fulfilling. There are, after all, no outward consequences to deal with since your issue is between you and God, distinguishing it from sexual activity involving another person. The sin issue is not so apparent here, as the Bible explicitly condemns homosexual *lust and behavior* rather than homosexual *orientation*. Christ's prohibition against lust (Matthew 5:28) certainly applies to the entertaining of sexual fantasies and erotic desires outside of marriage, but not to the condition of homosexuality. A heterosexual male is attracted to women, but he is not always lusting after them. Likewise, a homosexual male is attracted to men, but he is not always lusting after them.

So if to you "status quo" means repeatedly confessing to God your episodes of lust and resisting erotic temptations, you could go the rest of your life maintaining it. No one will know unless you want them to; it's your secret.

But is it worth keeping? Remember the high cost of secrecy: isolation and the resulting avoidance of whatever help may be available. Isolation, whether it's the isolation of a person or an issue, is never healthy. Like expanding leaven, it infects the entire personality. So when James admonished us, "Confess your trespasses to one another, and pray for one another, that you may be healed" (James 5:16), he was prescribing an act of spiritual and therapeutic value.

Consider Holocaust survivor Corrie ten Boom, bestselling author, subject of the book and film *The Hiding Place*, and clearly one of the most remarkable Christian leaders of the past century. During her imprisonment in the Ravensbruck concentration camp (her "crime" was protecting Jewish Hollanders from the Nazis), she noticed a gradual hardening of her heart toward fellow inmates. She became protective of what few possessions she had and developed a withdrawn, self-centered attitude. It's almost laughable to think that, in the midst of a death camp, she was concerned about her attitude. And yet, she recalls, her private conflict began to affect her energy and zeal, both of which were crucial to her survival:

> The special temptation of concentration-camp life—the temptation to think only of oneself, took a thousand cunning forms. I knew this was self-centered, and even if it wasn't right, it wasn't so very wrong, was it? Not wrong like sadism and

murder and the other monstrous evils we saw every day.

Was it coincidence that joy and power drained from my ministry? My prayers took on a mechanical ring. Bible study reading was dull and lifeless, so I struggled on with worship and teaching that had ceased to be real. Until one afternoon when the truth blazed like sunlight in the shadows. And so I told the group of women around me the truth about myself—my self-centeredness, my stinginess, my lack of love. That night real joy returned to my worship.[1]

Disclosure was a release for Corrie, the benefit of which is attested to in numerous Christian and secular studies. Especially revealing is the connection Dr. John White makes between self-disclosure and sexual healing. Speaking to the Christian beset with homosexual longings, he says:

> You are not despicable. You were made in the image of God. That image in you may have been defaced, yet it is still there. And a defaced master-piece is better by far than the unspoiled statue of a third-rate artist. But you will never feel this way about yourself until you take the risk of exposing your inner self—of revealing what you are ashamed of—to someone else. What you need is to warm your soul in the sunshine of another person's respect and understanding and in so doing begin to rediscover respect for yourself. If your problem is not too deeply ingrained, this of itself may be enough to begin to set you free.[2]

So James's advice to disclose our faults one to another has been reaffirmed by modern-day saints and theorists. Disclosure opens the door to intimate communication and support from the people we choose to admit our weaknesses to, and so begins the flow of emotional healing.

We can assume, if your struggle is exclusively inward, you can maintain the status quo and reap the benefit of private safety. The consequence of that decision is isolation, anxiety, and the probability that nothing will change.

If you are sexually active outside of marriage, then your struggle is not just between you and God. One or several other people are directly involved, and by allowing the situation to continue you are maintaining a deadly status quo with far-reaching, possibly irreversible consequences. Your decision at this point—whether or not to take action—will shape the direction and definition of your life. (For clarification's sake I will define "sexually active outside of marriage" to mean engaging in any form of sexual activity with another person outside of marriage.)

You may feel the payoff for sexual activity outweighs the consequences. But if you think ahead, as any wise person building his life must do, you will realize that while the payoff is temporary, the consequences are eternal. Although sin can be forgiven, its effects may continue their destructive course indefinitely.

The televangelist scandals of the late 1980s underscore this point. Who would have guessed that ministers of international stature were involved in sexual behavior the average Christian wouldn't even consider? All the more significant is the fact their ministries continued to flourish long before their private sins were exposed.

Regarding sexual sin, two points stand out. First, it won't just "go away." It requires the light of confession and accountability if it is to be overcome. Secrecy was a common element in those scandals; that's usually the case. Sin confessed is sin forgiven, but sin covered up becomes a throbbing, festering entity of its own, exacting a high price of guilt and the fear of being caught. It is exhausting to keep hiding something, but if you're unwilling to bring it to light, hiding is your only other option. Eventually, though, the problem will become too big and complicated to hide any longer.

Second, and perhaps more important, repetitive sin becomes a taskmaster rather than a pleasure. You may have comforted yourself so far with the notion you're "getting away with it." But count on it: As long as anything in your life continues to be uncontrollable, you're in bondage to it. For now, the bondage itself is its own consequence. To maintain the status quo means not only to remain sexually active, but also to remain under the control of secretive behavior that you neither want nor believe in. If you doubt the need to take action by allowing a fellow believer to walk through this struggle with you, ask yourself one question: If you could overcome this on your own, why haven't you?

Remember, God gives a certain space for repentance before He allows a catastrophe to come as an intervention. But if need be, He eventually lifts His protective hand to allow tragedy, if it is necessary for a person's restoration. Now may be your "space for repentance," a time for changing the status quo, not maintaining it. Don't delude yourself into assuming that this grace period will go on indefinitely. It didn't go on indefinitely for the world in Noah's time, nor will it for you. God is still no respecter of persons.

Abandoning the Faith

By now you may be contemplating a complete departure from Christianity. Having tried, perhaps for years, to overcome homosexual desires, you may feel the struggle is ferocious and the payoffs minimal. "Backsliding" looks like the only option, because it seems you ultimately have to choose between being a homosexual and being a Christian.

But that sort of reasoning would logically lead everyone in the church to backslide as well, because all Christians deal with sin, all Christians have stubborn areas of weakness, and all Christians at times feel overwhelmed by their personal issues. (Don't forget Paul's "O wretched man that I am!" lamentation in Romans 7.) Yet all Christians don't feel as though they have to completely overcome their weaknesses or else abandon the faith.

Still, it may seem to you that homosexual longings are in a problem class of their own, immune to your best efforts. That being the case, you may think your only hope of fulfillment lies in leaving Christ and embracing homosexuality because, God knows, you have tried to change but you just can't.

The immediate payoff for such a decision is gratification. You may be able to find some satisfaction in a homosexual relationship—perhaps for a season, perhaps longer. It's useless to paint a morbid picture of such relationships just for the sake of dissuading you. You will find out for yourself. The point here is that, should you abandon your faith and indulge your passions, you will no longer be denying yourself the "right" to do what seems natural to you. And that may really seem more important to you than Christianity itself.

But then what *is* your concept of Christianity? Before you consider abandoning it, consider whether you really understood it in the first place. Crucial to your understanding is the way you might answer the following questions: Did God promise you that, having been converted, you would be finished with personal struggles? While it's true that Christ promised us an abundant life, does "abundant" mean "perfect, without any trials, loneliness, or deprivation"? Is Christianity simply a religious form of therapy designed to ensure the happiness of its followers?

Does it make you angry to even ask these questions? If so, you may have forgotten that the core of our faith is the Person Jesus Christ, and the expression of our faith is a life of service to Him, not ourselves.

Francis Schaeffer describes the Christian life in terms of "positives" and "negatives" in his thoughtful book *True Spirituality* (Tyndale House, 1971). Schaeffer feels that, before considering the more "positive" aspects of the faith, we need to identify ourselves with Christ in His death ("not my will but Thine be done") as well as in His resurrection— the "negative" preceding the "positive."

This principle especially holds true when applied to homosexuality. It seems people attracted to individuals of the same sex experience three common phases after their conversion: an initial phase of idealism ("I'm free! It's all in the past!"), a disturbing plateau of lingering sexual issues ("I'm waiting for my deliverance."), and a period of disillusionment ("So where's the deliverance? Will I ever really change?"). That is the point at which crucial decisions are made, and it is at *that* point, I feel, that identification with Christ's death and a commitment to godly living in spite of unresolved sexual issues must take priority over the desire for change. Only then does real growth come—when the desire for change is secondary to the desire to obey.

In short, Christianity is not something you "try" to see if it solves your problems. Rather, it's a personal relationship with God made available through Christ and is evidenced by a willingness to serve Him on His terms, not ours: "If anyone desires to come after Me, let him deny himself, and take up his cross, and follow Me" (Matthew 16:24).

Regarding our attitude toward this primary but overlooked aspect of Christianity, Schaeffer comments:

> So I must ask, very gently: How much thought does [our identification with Christ's death] provoke? Is it not true that our thoughts, our prayers for ourselves and those we love, are almost entirely aimed at getting rid of the negative, at any cost—rather than praying that the negatives might be faced in the proper attitude?[3]

Regarding sexual practices, he becomes even more specific:

> Here, in the midst of life, there is to be a strong negative, by choice, and by the grace of God. It is not, for example, a matter of waiting until we no longer have strong sexual desires, but rather that in the midst of the moving of life, surrounded by a world that grabs everything, we are to understand what Jesus means when He talks about denying ourselves that which is not rightfully ours.[4]

We shouldn't leave it at that. There *is* more to Christianity than "the negatives"—infinitely more. It begins with the eternal life we enter into at the moment of salvation and the honor of knowing and loving God—an honor that must cause us real shame when we consider our preoccupation with our temporary struggles. Inherent in our relationship with God is the privilege of addressing our needs to a loving Father (Matthew 6:7,8), who gives us either the things we request or the grace to deal with our lack (2 Corinthians 12:8,9). A morbid preoccupation with self-denial is not desirable. In fact, it can become as idolatrous as an obsession with self-fulfillment.

But Schaeffer's point is worth our attention. True fulfillment for the Christian can come only after a surrender of ourselves to God's larger purposes and a commitment to holy living, whether or not it comes "naturally" to us. That is Christian living. If you're going to abandon it, at least know what it is you're abandoning. You're not walking away from a God who let you down; you're probably walking away from a faith you misunderstood.

One more point to consider: Abandoning the faith in a quest for personal happiness may well be the way to sabotage that very quest. Remember, if you are a believer, you have experienced the rebirth described in John 3:16, which is not easily shrugged off. You were given the seed of God Himself: "Having been born again, not of corruptible seed but incorruptible, through the word of God" (1 Peter 1:23).

This generates a new nature: "If anyone is in Christ, he is a new creation; old things have passed away; behold, all things have become new" (2 Corinthians 5:17). This in turn cannot be fulfilled when violating God's own standards: "How shall we who died to sin live any longer in it?" (Romans 6:2).

That being the case, it's questionable whether you will ever be happy in a backslidden state. The dissatisfaction you will feel apart from fellowship with Christ may well outweigh whatever dissatisfaction you're experiencing now as a struggling Christian.

You might argue, "But I am who I am—a homosexual. That's my nature, and I can't be at peace unless I'm true to myself."

I would argue the same point, changing the noun. You are indeed who you are—a Christian. That's your nature, and you can't be at peace unless you're true to yourself.

Compromising Scriptural Standards

The past few decades have witnessed a form of compromise that has generated confusion and controversy in equal proportions. Promoters of this option insist the traditional biblical view of homosexuality is obsolete and should be replaced with a reevaluation of Scripture which yields, in essence, the following conclusion:

1. There is no biblical condemnation of homosexual behavior so long as it occurs within the boundaries of a "loving, committed relationship."

2. Scriptures commonly supposed to condemn homosexual acts instead condemn only homosexual *lust* or *irresponsible* homosexual behavior.

3. The words commonly translated to mean "homosexual" are generally mistranslated and should be taken to mean either "idolaters," "homosexual prostitutes," or "cowardly people." (See Appendix 3, "Pro-Gay Theology," for a more detailed discussion of the Bible and homosexuality.)

The option opened up by such beliefs is to fully accept and act upon homosexual desires *and* remain a Bible-believing Christian. You can fellowship in a church that openly celebrates same-sex relationships (there are many such churches) and continue to identify yourself as a born-again Christian. In a sense, this new option isn't new at all. In Revelation 2:14-16 Jesus rebuked the church at Pergamos for holding to the "doctrine of Balaam," which, He said, He held against them. Essentially, this doctrine is derived from the events described in Numbers 22 and 31, in which the prophet Balaam, unable to curse God's people Israel, instead counseled them to compromise themselves through sexual immorality with the Moabites. They retained their identification as God's people, it should be noted, but their compromised holiness had serious repercussions. Jesus identified the believers at Pergamos as being His people, even commending them for their strong points (Revelation 2:13). But the issue was compromise—something which was unacceptable to the Head of the church (Revelation 2:16).

But to other segments of the church and society it is perfectly acceptable. If you have not yet considered this option, be assured that at some point it will present itself to you. Before accepting it at face value, consider the short-term benefits in light of the long-range consequences.

An immediate benefit is the sense of having what looks like the best of both worlds: an openly gay identity (no more struggle!) plus a fellowship of believers supporting and even celebrating the very thing you have sought so long to deny. That in itself can be such a powerful experience, it may lead you to believe it's a literal godsend.

It is also possible that your relationship with God will remain intact. (Although your *fellowship* with Him will be seriously injured.) The very notion that a person could practice homosexuality and remain saved may raise some eyebrows, but Christians can and do sin. Remember that the Corinthian believers, in spite of remarkable ungodliness (incest, drunkenness during communion, serious factions) still enjoyed a manifestation of the Holy Spirit in their assembly (1 Corinthians 12 and 14). So you, if you choose this option, may still enjoy a measure of spiritual experience and gifts which are, after all, given without change of mind on God's part (Romans 11:29). Perhaps that, too, will convince you of the rightness of your choice.

The serious drawback to this option lies in its misrepresentation of Scripture and its unwillingness to accept scriptural authority as absolute. A telling illustration is provided in a pro-gay autobiography which chronicles the expansion of the Metropolitan Community churches. Explaining his church's interpretation of the Bible and the factors influencing that interpretation, the author states, "What influences led us to new ways of understanding Scriptures? New scientific information, social changes and personal experience are perhaps the greatest forces for change in the way we interpret the Bible and develop our beliefs."[5]

To this Francis Schaeffer in *The Great Evangelical Disaster* aptly replies, "First one starts questioning, based on what the world around us is saying, then one looks at Scripture, then theology, then scientific study—until finally what the Scriptures teach is completely subjected to whatever view is currently accepted by the world."[6]

It is impossible to tamper with one portion of Scripture without compromising all of it. This is not just an academic problem, but a dangerous error that can only lead to further compromise in all areas of life and doctrine.

To choose this option is to do more than accept an altered interpretation of Scripture. It is to participate in deception and ultimately to become its victim. The compromise that paves the way for deception never stops at one issue but is characterized by a continued hardening of the heart. And make no mistake about this: No believer, however earnest, is immune to deception and eventual catastrophe when he allows compromise to go unchecked. King Solomon's revelation of God was notable, his calling as king verified by specific visitations. But he had his weaknesses, turning his heart toward lovers who worshiped other gods and who would eventually turn his heart from Jehovah (1 Kings 11:1-8). It would seem as though his idolatry began with simple compromise in one area—liaisons with the ungodly—which grew into overt rebellion. Compromise invites idolatry; idolatry evolves into apostasy. In Scripture, as in life, no downhill course is complete until the bottom is reached.

You are here, you are not alone, and you are facing alternatives. You cannot make intelligent choices without dealing with them. If your choice is the option detailed in this book—repentance of all homosexual activity and earnest seeking for sexual wholeness—know that it is in many ways a difficult one. Difficult and wonderful, because your willingness to deal with your sexuality will increase your understanding of so many human issues. Most important, as one who was given the responsibility to steward his body and soul and who did so to the best of his ability, you become a candidate for a blessed pronouncement that few will hear: "Well done, thou good and faithful servant; thou hast been faithful over a few things, I will make thee ruler over many things: enter thou into the joy of thy lord" (Matthew 25:21 KJV).

Afterthoughts on
You Are Here

Since I had already tried three of the options mentioned in this chapter—maintaining the status quo, abandoning the faith, and compromising biblical standards—the only one left for me in 1984 was repentance. And no matter what difficulties and struggles have been involved, I have never regretted my decision. Initially, I did it out of obedience. Only later would I realize how much personal satisfaction it would bring me. What I thought I was doing for God was, in fact, the greatest favor I ever did myself.

That's probably why, when I originally wrote this chapter, I was naive enough to think most men who started on this course would stay on it. Today, I can't even estimate the number I have known who have turned their backs on this option. Their choices are their own, of course, and must be respected. But I reserve the right to weep over what I can only see as tragedy and waste.

A year before writing this update, one of the more well-known, up-and-coming ministers in the southern California area was found to have been involved with a male parishioner. Evidently he had known of his attraction to men but chose to believe it was a nonissue—one that need not involve counsel or accountability. He chose the status quo, and we all lost as a result. God knows (and I'm sure we will, too) how many similar stories are churning just beneath the surface today, ready to erupt into yet another scandal, another wound.

I have also seen too many believers walk away from Christ altogether, either out of disillusionment with the church (sometimes justifiable, sometimes an excuse) or refusal to accept the idea of Lordship over their sexuality. I have gotten scathing letters from men and women who had repented of homosexuality, then returned to it, violently rejecting Christianity in the process.

Sometimes they spew out hatred for me and other "ex-gays," blaming us for encouraging them to change without telling them how hard (or impossible, they say) change really is. Sometimes they rail at God and His "unfairness" for letting them feel so strongly attracted to the same sex, then forbidding them to gratify those attractions. So they choose another god who will be more user-friendly, but the unhappiness of that choice is betrayed in their bitter tone. Is there anyone more desolate than the man who has known Christ, tasted eternity, then thrown it all away?

But no one is more critical of this book's approach than those who identify themselves as "gay Christians." Browse the Internet and you will find countless web sites dedicated to promoting the "Gay is okay with God" theory. Many of them, you will notice, are manned by people who tried to do what you're doing, then decided God didn't require it of them. By now I've lost my ability to be shocked at believers' willingness to kid themselves into the "gay Christian" myth. I did it myself, after all. But 12 years ago I didn't in my worst nightmares anticipate the level of support, both religious and secular, for such an enormous compromise of Scripture and basic integrity.

Yeah, I was naive about a lot of things. But not about this: I knew there would always be guys like you who would settle for nothing less than truth, who would put obedience above satisfaction, who would walk this way. I was right about that.

I'm not right often enough, but when I am, I really do love it.

Motivation and Expectations

Leading up to a decisive choice for sexual purity, we must make some hard choices and answer some hard questions: How long do I intend to stay ensnared? How long must my family wait? How long before I can look God in the eye?

—FROM *EVERY MAN'S BATTLE* BY
STEPHEN ARTERBURN AND FRED STOEKER

One of my first questions to a counselee wanting to change is "Why?" Sometimes that earns me a "Dumb question, buddy" kind of look. "I'm a Christian" is the usual answer, "and Christians aren't supposed to be gay! Isn't it obvious why I want to change?"

Not necessarily. The fact that someone wants to do the right thing doesn't mean he wants to do it for the right reason. Proper motivation is essential to success. Plenty of Christians want to do the right thing for the wrong reasons. Some of us are driven to evangelize friends and coworkers out of a sense of guilt ("Good Christians witness, you know!") rather than out of concern for their souls. Lots of us tithe for a tax write-off, dropping our checks into the offering plate with no thought toward God. And how many pastors are motivated by a need for recognition rather than a love for their flock? Doing the right thing is one matter; *why* you are doing it is another.

You might argue that your reason for wanting to change is irrelevant, because your desire to change is enough to guarantee success. Not so. Your motivation needs to be clarified now, at the beginning, because it will determine your consistency and perseverance along the way. Suppose you knew two men who were 40 pounds overweight. Both of them decided to diet, but for different reasons. One man wants to look better, while the other has a heart condition and has been warned by his doctor that his life is endangered by his obesity. They both want to do the same thing, but different factors are motivating them. Whom are you going to put your money on?

Let me put it more plainly. I have seen many Christian men struggling with homosexuality who decide they want to "go straight." Thank God, I have seen plenty of successes. But there are plenty of failures, too. And among the failures I have seen two common elements: wrong motivation and unrealistic expectations.

A Poor Prognosis

A prognosis is the prospect of recovery, whether physical or emotional, made by the person treating a certain condition. The prognosis is based on several factors, including the normal course of the condition, special circumstances, past history, and so forth. So a physician, when asked to give a prognosis for a patient with terminal cancer, will probably give a poor prognosis, meaning that the prospect of recovery is slim.

In counseling, I consider motivation (among many other things) when making a prognosis. In all cases motives are important, but I pay special attention to the reasons people say they want help with homosexuality. Opening statements in counseling sessions say a lot, often revealing the real reason(s) the counselee came in.

Take as an example the young man who says, "I'm here for my parents." This is always a bad sign, especially coming from an adult. Often well-meaning parents send their adult daughters or sons into counseling because they (the parents) want their kids to get "straightened out." The kids themselves may be perfectly satisfied with their orientation, but they don't want to upset their families. Or they are afraid of being written out of their parents' wills. Or their parents are putting them through college, and they don't want to jeopardize future tuition payments. And so, under mild (or blatant) coercion, these young men and women come to counseling saying, in essence, "I don't mind being homosexual, but my parents can't stand it, so here I am!"

Now, I'm not unsympathetic to the feelings of parents who find out about their offspring's homosexuality. The discovery is usually a shock, creating upheaval and heartache. But nobody can expect to change just because someone else wants him to. And, in my opinion, nobody should even attempt this sort of change if his heart isn't in it.

So let me ask you candidly: For whom are you doing this? Do you personally feel that homosexuality is unnatural, that you cannot be satisfied with your sexual leanings, and that to act on them would cause you guilt because you believe such actions are wrong? If not, reexamine your own beliefs and make your own decision. *You cannot expect any measure of success unless you yourself want to change.*

Fear of Hell

"I'm afraid of going to hell" is another reason often cited. And hell is something to fear, to be sure. It is a literal, specific horror which Jesus warned us about in graphic detail. You can't take the Bible seriously without feeling a certain dread and sadness when the subject of hell comes up.

But homosexuality is not a "heaven or hell" issue. Nobody goes to heaven because he is heterosexual; nobody goes to hell because he is homosexual. Eternal judgment is based on one thing: whether or not your name is recorded in the Book of Life to be opened at the last judgment (Revelation 20:1-15). Through faith in Christ apart from our own righteousness, we can expect to see our names on the record. Whoever will, as Paul said, confess Jesus Christ with his mouth and believe in his heart that God has raised Him from the dead will be saved (Romans 10:9).

A "reformed homosexual" is no more a candidate for heaven than a drug addict who gives up dope or a thief who quits stealing. While all of these are good, admirable reforms, neither they nor any works of righteousness we do can bring us one whit closer to glory. It is Christ's work alone which made provision for our salvation, not any reformation on our part. If you fear hell, go back to the basics: "God so loved the world that He gave His only begotten Son, that whoever believes in Him should not perish but have everlasting life" (John 3:16).

Even after we have been born again into that eternal life, we remain in earthly bodies with earthly struggles. The question for the Christian, then, is not whether or not his struggles will doom him to hell (they won't), but rather how he can best overcome his struggles because, as a child of God, he has been born to higher purposes.

If you are a child of God, you are not condemned to hell because of your struggles or your sin. So don't "go straight" to try to become a child of God; rather, abandon sin because you already are a child of God.

Does that mean the believer can indulge in homosexual behavior because, no matter what, he remains a child of God and will not be eternally punished for it? Never—just the opposite, in fact. A true believer cannot continue willfully in any sin without suffering consequences. Willful sin goes against the true nature of anyone belonging to Christ (Romans 6:1-4) and can only lead to misery in the long run. But to give up any sin for the sake of avoiding hell is to miss the main point. Through Christ, God has already made provision for us to escape hell in spite of our sins. We overcome sin, then, out of gratitude to and love for God, not to avoid His eternal judgment.

Change as Experiment...or Commitment

"I want to try going straight to see if it works" is a reason some men offer as their motivation for change.

But what if it doesn't "work"? Are you saying that either way of life would be okay with you? You would "prefer" heterosexuality, but you're keeping the homosexual option open?

In that case, your interest in change sounds more like an experiment than a commitment. And commitment, not curious dabbling, is needed before any major changes can happen.

Which brings us to a proper and reasonable motivation: a desire to change based on ethics and beliefs, and a commitment to abstain from what is known to be unethical and seek what is known to be healthy and right. All arguments for or against homosexuality get down to questions of ethics: Is homosexuality normal or abnormal, moral or immoral, an orientation God intended for some people or a perversion of normal sexuality?

We are prone to back ourselves into corners when we stray beyond these questions, or when we have no objective standard to answer them by. For example, the conservative who argues that "homosexuality is obviously abnormal because homosexuals are promiscuous, irrational, and violent people" is setting himself up to get shot down. It can be proved that many homosexuals are not promiscuous, and that violence and irrational behavior are common to all people, homosexual and heterosexual alike. So his argument loses its strength because it's based on a debatable point. The question is not whether a person can be nice, responsible, and lovable while being homosexual (a person can, of course, and many gays are very likable people), but whether or not homosexuality is normal *in and of itself*, and whether or not homosexual acts *in and of themselves* are ever moral.

To answer this question requires an analysis of beliefs about sexuality in general and a determination of what we base our beliefs on. If we have no objective standard to judge these things by, then arguments against homosexuality are weak. If morality is relative after all, why shouldn't consenting adults do as they please with either sex? Who is to say that attractions to the same sex are unhealthy if there is no objective standard of healthy sexuality? For that matter, who is to say what the "Christian" view is if there's not even an objective standard for Christian beliefs?

Of course, such a standard exists in the Bible, which is the final test on all matters of belief and morality. The Bible provides concrete answers that are not subject to change or reinterpretation. That's how our beliefs and ethics as Christians are defined: I believe a thing to be right or wrong, moral or immoral, based on the biblical viewpoint of it. That finally determines what practices and kinds of relationships I can engage in.

If homosexuality is defined as *unnatural* in the Scriptures (it is—check Romans 1), then if I experience homosexual desires I must conclude they are unnatural, even if they *feel* natural to me. Any number of abnormalities may feel natural. If we have no standard other than our feelings, then any mood or proclivity we experience can be called "normal."

If homosexual acts are described as immoral in the Scriptures (as they are in Romans 1 and 1 Corinthians 6), then I have to conclude that any form of homosexual behavior, whether in the context of a one-night stand or a 30-year monogamous relationship, is immoral no matter how right or good the behavior may seem. Again, the standard is Scripture, not experience or feelings.

And if I am a Christian, I cannot allow unnatural tendencies or immoral actions to dominate my life. Otherwise I can never be truly at peace, nor can I reach my potential in Christ.

Motivation that lends itself to a good prognosis might be articulated as follows:

> Because I believe, based on biblical standards, that my homosexual desires are unnatural and that homosexual behavior is immoral, and because I know that to continue in any form of immorality will displease the God I love while inhibiting my spiritual and emotional growth, I am committed to abstaining from homosexual acts and am equally committed to doing anything I can to become sexually whole.

Great Expectations

Having made that commitment, what sort of changes can you expect to happen?

Expectations, like motivation, have much to do with success. When people expect too much too soon, they become disillusioned and quit. So let me emphasize the importance of being realistic. Hopeful, *yes*. Confident in God's work in you, *definitely*. But never naive or blindly optimistic. I stress this because men are often plagued by magical thinking. They assume that, having done all the "right things," their sexual struggles will vanish and normal attractions will take their place...completely...by next Tuesday.

Compounding the problem, they may tell themselves that they are healed long before their healing is a reality, supposing that presumption is faith. With a Christian Science sort of mentality they repeat their mantra: "I'm changed. I'm delivered. I'm straight." And when they are sexually tempted they say, "That's not a homosexual desire. It's just a lie of the devil." Their intentions are good, but their theology allows no room for slow growth. When they are finally weary of telling themselves that what *is* really *is not*, they give up the fight.

Don't let that be said of you. Define your expectations, keeping them reasonable and biblically based.

So what sort of changes can you expect? Let's break the subject down by addressing the questions men in your position often pose.

Is it possible for a person who is attracted to the same sex to ever be completely free of those attractions and never experience them again? Certainly it's possible, but very unlikely. The same can be said of any human tendencies. We all come to Christ with a variety of psychological problems. We commit ourselves to discipleship, trusting in the process of sanctification to bring us closer and closer to His image. As Paul said, "We all, with unveiled face, beholding as in a mirror the glory of the Lord, are being transformed into the same image from glory to glory, just as by the Spirit of the Lord" (2 Corinthians

3:18). From glory to glory—that's process. Further on he says, "We who are in this tent [our earthly bodies] groan, being burdened" (2 Corinthians 5:4).

There is *struggle* during the process, no question about it. Does that mean we never change? Of course not; we change significantly. The power that our sins have had over us is broken; we no longer have to give in to them. Their influence over us is felt less and less; it is present, perhaps, but not predominant. Our perspective changes as we realize that we are living with the hope of eternal life and that although we are beset by sin to some degree, we are no longer its slaves. These are principles that apply to all Christians, no matter what problems they battle.

Homosexuality is no different. Like all sinful tendencies, homosexual attractions need not rule you or continue to be a predominant force in your life. Specifically, you can expect change to occur in one or all of four ways. (In chapter 6 we will take up the "change" question more fully.)

1. *Change in behavior.* Some people argue that behavioral change isn't really change at all. But they're wrong. When a person's behavior changes, his life changes. If a man has been a drunkard for 20 years, then joins Alcoholics Anonymous and stays sober, he has definitely changed. His sobriety will have an impact on all parts of his life, improving his attitude, relationships, and job performance. Will an occasional desire for a drink nullify his claim to have changed? Hardly. So it is with you. If you have been homosexually active and reach a point of consistent sexual sobriety, you will have changed. Conscience, confidence, and self-control will all have been affected by your abstinence. There is no area of your life that will not feel the impact of it.

2. *Change in frequency of homosexual attractions.* One of the first noticeable changes my clients report has to do with the

frequency of their attractions. Generally, they notice they are less often aroused by persons of the same sex. They don't deny that it may still happen, but not nearly as much as it used to. And they're not walking around with their eyes closed, either. Their episodes of attraction to other men are significantly rarer than they used to be. You can realistically expect, then, to experience a reduction in the frequency of homosexual longings.

3. *Change in intensity of homosexual attractions.* Attractions will become less powerful, less intense, and easier to shrug off. That, too, is a major change. One male client put it this way: "I used to be overwhelmed with lust when I'd see a good-looking guy. Now I look, and I'll notice the fact that he's handsome, but I don't feel nearly as turned on as I used to. If I do get aroused, which happens less and less, it's not so strong. It used to be 'WOW!' Now it's 'oh.'"

4. *Change in perspective.* Some people are so obsessed with their homosexuality that their obsession is a bigger problem than their attractions. Healing for these people begins when they realize that same-sex lust isn't the end of the world. They see it for what it really is: just another manifestation of the fallen nature. The difference between obsession with homosexuality and acknowledgment of it as a nuisance but not a catastrophe, is a change you can also expect to happen.

Is it possible for someone like me to ever have sexual attractions to the opposite sex? Yes, it is possible. But the probability of heterosexual desires either emerging or returning depends, to a large extent, on your sexual history. Some people have always been exclusively homosexual, never having had attractions to the opposite sex. Other individuals have had, to different degrees, heterosexual attractions which have coexisted with homosexual ones. Of course, the person who has had heterosexual attractions in the past is more *likely* to experience them than the person who has never experienced them in the first place. But even that may be an oversimplification. There are studies which report remarkable changes in orientation, even among those who were predominantly homosexual (see chapter 6). So in general, yes, heterosexual attractions are possible. My opinion, in fact, is that the potential for heterosexuality exists in all people, so that heterosexual response can be awakened in even a predominantly homosexual person.

Once I do experience changes, would it ever be possible for me to go back into homosexual relationships? Yes. We can all go back to wherever we have been. Under certain circumstances, anyone can regress or backslide. That does not mean you will be forever hanging onto your sexual wholeness for dear life. It just means that, like anyone else, you can go backward or forward. That does not mean your changes were not real.

Look at Peter's life. He careened from cowardliness to boldness at different times. He was quite the warrior when he swore he would never deny Christ, and even more so when the soldiers arrested Jesus in the garden and Peter drew his sword, whacking off a man's ear. His aggression was short-lived, however, when that same night he pretended not even to know Christ rather than risk his own arrest through association with Him. Then he flip-flopped again in the book of Acts, boldly accusing the people in Jerusalem of murdering Christ—the same people he evidently feared earlier. When he was cowardly, did that mean he was never really bold? Of course not. But in some situations he became weak and regressed.

So can you. I am convinced that anyone who has had homosexual experiences can, under certain conditions, be homosexually tempted. That does not mean such a person *will* be tempted. Some people who have been homosexually oriented in the past claim to now have no attractions at all to the same sex and no desire for any kind of homosexual contact. (While I have not personally witnessed that sort of change in sexuality, I certainly don't dismiss its possibility.) But the possibility of those desires returning later in life is always there. To expect differently is to be very unrealistic indeed. However, the more you grow, the less likely such a regression will be.

Expect to grow. Expect your homosexual desires to diminish in both their frequency and their intensity. Expect your perspective to change radically as you expand your vision and reach your potential. These expectations form a proper, realistic, and hopeful viewpoint of the growth process. Combined with a motivation born of love and dissatisfaction with anything less than God's best, they provide you with the inner resources you will be needing.

Defining your motives and expectations make the process easier. So far we have examined inward issues—beliefs, influences, and so forth. Now is the time to begin taking action.

Afterthoughts on
Motivation and Expectations

Okay, maybe that was a long-winded way of saying, "This is gonna be hard." And I really didn't think you assumed it would be easy. But it's crucial to have already settled in your mind *why* you're doing this, and *what* you expect to happen as a result.

Most of the men I've known who didn't make it seemed to be unclear on one or both of these points.

This shows up when a man says, "I never lost the attractions to men," or "I never found the right kind of help," or "No one in the church understood me/liked me/accepted me/sought me out."

"So," they say, "I *quit!*" Which is another way of saying, "I tried to go straight because I figured I would become turned on to women, find the sort of help I've always wanted, and be warmly accepted and understood by the Christian community." All of which doesn't mix well with the Lord's description of life with Him as being one of sacrifice, cross-bearing, and being hated by the world.

So if no one else has done so, let me help you lower your expectations.

My wife says I'm too cynical; that I can't handle disappointment, so I always assume the worst, which protects me from being let down. And she's right, but in this case it's okay, because there is no point in continuing this journey without starkly realistic expectations.

You may never lose the attractions to men. I think—and experience has shown—that they will fade, so they certainly will not rule you. But complete transformation without temptation? Not likely. Count on some level of testing, and count on it continuing for life.

While you're at it, count on being misunderstood, misinterpreted, even mistreated at times. Back in August 1998, *Newsweek's* cover story, "Gay For Life," featured the experiences of men like you. Typically pro-gay, the article expressed doubt over the possibility of a homosexual changing, but the writer was dead-on when he said, "Few identities in America are more marginal than ex-gay." Marginal indeed. Much of our culture thinks we're either deluded or in denial; many in our churches think we're fundamentally flawed.

So why bother? Besides the obvious—obedience in this life, rewards in the next—this struggle takes us to the basics of Christianity, perhaps in ways few can know. Maybe, more than most people, we can appreciate the severity of the conflict between flesh and spirit. Maybe our struggle creates in us a reliance on God we would never know otherwise. And this I *can* promise: Going through this process gives you an appreciation for human frailty *and* human potential that is priceless.

I hate my past, but I love what it has brought about in me. That's not too cynical, is it?

Three
Repentance

When you're angry enough, scared enough, or frustrated
enough, you take action. So it is with homosexuality. If you're
ready to repent of homosexual sin, you're probably angry ("I've
had it!"), scared ("God, be merciful to me a sinner!"), or feeling the futility of it all ("There's no future in this for me!").
All three roads lead to repentance.

To repent is to turn. That's what distinguishes repentance
from confession, which is a simple acknowledgment of sin
as opposed to actively turning from it. It is through confession, according to 1 John 1:9, that we are forgiven of sin: "If
we confess our sins, He is faithful and just to forgive us our
sins and to cleanse us from all unrighteousness."

But confession doesn't necessarily change us, important
as it is. God not only calls us to acknowledge our sin. He
also commands us to put it away.

Now *repent* is a word we associate with dour men in sack-cloth warning us about the coming doom. That's too bad, because repentance is a valuable concept. It means "to think differently, reconsider, turn around." No real changes are made without it. Repentance is the willful act of discontinuing a thing which is destructive, followed by an earnest effort to do what is constructive and right.

Without confession, nothing is forgiven; but without repentance, nothing is changed.

Repent of What?

To repent, or turn, you need to first identify what you are repenting of, then determine the most effective way to do it. Exactly what do you need to repent of? That depends on exactly how you are expressing homosexual desires.

Of course you can't repent of *having* those desires. You can't rip them out and abandon them, and you can't just will them away. Repentance applies only to acts of the *conscious will*, whether they are outward actions or inward indulgences. So you are not trying to repent of *homosexuality* per se but of *conscious homosexual expressions.*

Outward expressions of homosexuality include sexual contact, erotic noncontact behavior (exhibitionism, telephone sex), and the use of pornography. These are direct forms of immoral behavior, easy to detect and obviously immoral.

Less obvious but also immoral are indirect expressions, such as conscious lusting or sexual fantasies. Although these practices are inward, they are still conscious expressions since they involve an act of the will. Conscious lusting is the indulgence of sexual desires for another person. It should be distinguished from an attraction, although the line which distinguishes the two is indeed a fine one. An attraction occurs when a person gets your attention, arouses you, and causes an erotic response.

("Wow, that guy's good-looking; he turns me on," etc.) Lust, on the other hand, occurs when you feed that attraction by focusing on it, elaborating on it ("I would love to do this or that with him") or, as some say, "Undressing him with your eyes." To be attracted is no sin; to deliberately fuel that attraction is.

Sexual fantasies are similar. They, like sexual lust, are conscious acts of the imagination. And they, too, need to be distinguished from fleeting sexual thoughts. Martin Luther, speaking of impure thoughts, said that we can't keep the birds from flying over our heads, but we can keep them from building a nest in our hair. That is pretty well put. Wayward sexual thoughts come to everyone, I suppose, but when we indulge those thoughts by orchestrating sexual fantasies, then we're not just having fleeting thoughts; we're creating mental pornographic home movies.

All of these forms of homosexuality are so obvious that you probably didn't need me to point them out to you. But repentance shouldn't stop here. You should also consider any activities that contribute to them or encourage them. You need to be very honest with yourself. Are there parts of your lifestyle—habits, places you like to go, forms of recreation—that encourage sexual immorality? That's a question every Christian has to ask himself; it's a question that's doubly pertinent to you. So often, men can go on kidding themselves, then wonder why they're not making any progress. They claim to want freedom and seem willing to give up overt homosexual activity, but show an unwillingness to give up the very things that lead them back into that activity.

An old hangout—perhaps a local gay bar or nightclub—is a good example. It's possible to attend such a place without doing anything overtly wrong, but how does going there affect you? Does it stimulate lust, weaken your resolve, put you in an erotic frame of mind?

In all matters, the question should never be, "Is going to such and such a place an overt sin?" but rather, "Do I have the liberty to go to this place without setting myself up to stumble? Will it encourage me toward my goals, or will it encourage me toward a setback?"

Health clubs are another sore point for many people. Of course, there's nothing wrong with working out at a spa. In fact, it's a pretty healthy thing to do—but only if you can maintain your integrity while you do it. Plenty of men wrestling with homosexuality can barely (if at all) handle the atmosphere at a gym—the communal showers, the steam baths—without going into acute lust or, worse yet, getting into a sexual encounter. Again, the question isn't whether or not the thing itself is wrong, but whether or not it's wrong *for you*. "All things are lawful for me," Paul said, "but all things are not *helpful*" (1 Corinthians 6:12, emphasis added). In other words, like anyone serious about fulfilling a purpose, Paul weighed his actions against the effect they would have on his life goals.

So should you. Bring every part of your life under scrutiny. If anything you're involved with draws you toward the very thing you're trying to outgrow, drop it. That, in the truest sense, is repentance.

Roadblocks

There are two major stumbling blocks to repentance that you will have to fight: the love of the familiar and the fear of the unknown. Jesus makes an interesting reference to the love of the familiar when He refers to Himself as the "light which came into the world." People, He said, were in darkness and unable to comprehend the light when it came to them. That at least partially explains the rejection of Christ by His own people (John 1:11). But He takes it a step further and says that people were not only *in* darkness but that they actually *loved* it! (John 3:19). Their deeds were evil, and they had no desire to change. The comfort of their present state made them unwilling to consider any other way of life.

Never underestimate the power of the familiar. It has kept countless people from change, even when change would save their very lives. The familiar, after all, may be unhealthy, but at least we know it. We relate to it. And we are all too prone to cling to familiar territory.

When that "familiar territory" is sexual activity, it becomes perversely dear to us. Even though we admit it's wrong, we also come to see it as an old friend. It's reliable and available, and it works. It eases our pain and temporarily satisfies us. To repent of habitual sexual behavior can be like abandoning a trustworthy buddy.

Compare this to drug addiction. A person doesn't just fall into it. Somewhere along the line he discovers satisfaction through a chemical. It temporarily eases pain, helps him forget troubles, comforts him. It becomes his anesthetic, deadening his anxieties like a nurturing parent. Of course there are other ways he could deal with his problems, but the drug is familiar and has a good track record. Why give up something that works?

Meanwhile he is becoming addicted. What began as a comfort is now a necessity, emotionally and physically. To give it up means to go through physical withdrawal, which is hard enough. But it would also mean finding another way to cope with the inner conflicts which remain long after withdrawal. In fact, without the familiar coping mechanism formerly provided, those conflicts will be stronger and more painful than ever. The truth is, he *must* find other coping mechanisms, because the one he uses now will eventually destroy him.

God is the Author of legitimate need. He created us with the need for intimacy, bonding, love. If we, for whatever reason, do not get these needs met in the normal way, we will develop abnormal ways of satisfying them. Once these abnormal methods are part of our makeup, we're frightened to abandon them. Like faithful old friends, we rely on them and cannot imagine doing without them. In that sense we all love the familiar dark, not necessarily for its darkness, but for its familiarity.

So-called "adult bookstores" illustrate this. They are always there. You can call 20 of your friends in the middle of the night and they're likely to tell you to call back in the morning, but the porno shop doesn't care what time it is. It's reliable, familiar territory. And familiarity, no matter how destructive, is hard to abandon—it is the security blanket that smothers our good intentions.

Fear of the unknown is just as tough to beat. When we give up the familiar, we turn toward the unfamiliar. It may be to our benefit to do so, but it still threatens us. The unknown, no matter how good, is still the unknown. We have never been there, so we're not sure what to expect, nor are we certain what to do once we get there. At that point we long again for the comfort of the familiar.

Look at the Jewish people's journey out of Egypt. They had been in a terrible situation, cruelly driven to slave labor by their taskmasters. They lived in bondage and prayed for deliverance, and God intervened. He brought them out of Egypt miraculously and promised them a new start in a good land. And for a while that sounded great.

Then the exodus and the problems began. When faced with difficult situations in the wilderness, they were prone to long for the familiarity of Egypt and to dread the unknown Promised Land. Think about the power the familiar held for them! They had been treated worse than animals in Egypt, yet at times they would remember it fondly, saying, "At least we were fed regularly and had our basic needs taken care of!" The unknown frightened them, making them turn toward the bondage that they could at least relate to. And when they finally approached the Promised Land, the terror of its giant inhabitants overshadowed all the benefits that would go along with their new location. In Egypt at least they had survived. How could they be sure they would fare as well in new territory?

If you have met your primary emotional needs through homosexual behavior in the past, you may also wonder how you will fare in new territory. "If I could know that someday I'll feel as turned on to a woman as I do to a man," a client once told me, "this would be easier. Then it wouldn't be so hard to make all these changes, because I'd know someday it's all going to pay off. But when I look at straight couples and their kids, and think about me living that way and really enjoying it, I can't relate to it. I know where I want to be, but I can't even think of what it would be like to actually be there. And even if I do get there, how am I going to handle it?"

Your love of the familiar (homosexual practices) and fear of the unknown (repentance and a new life) will be alleviated when you consider the joy that the unknown holds for you. Sure, it's tough at times. But it also opens up a way of freedom, new relationships, and peace of mind. The good outweighs the bad immeasurably.

When the Israelites were finally ready to enter the land that God promised to bring them to, they sent out spies to see exactly what their new home would be like. Imagine the anticipation they were feeling! They didn't know much about this place—only that, whatever it was like, it had to be better than Egypt where they had been slaves, or the wilderness where they had wandered for so long. So they waited for the spies to return, having told them to bring back a sample of the fruit the land was bearing and a report on the kind of people who were already living there.

The spies returned with good news and bad news. The good news was that the fruit was abundant, a sure sign of healthy land. In fact, the grapes they brought back as a sample were so large that they had to be carried on a staff between two men! There was cause for real optimism and good reason to charge right in and take over.

The bad news was that there were also huge, intimidating giants dwelling in this unknown territory. The children of Israel appeared to be no match for these guys, who were so big that, according to the spies, they made the average man look like a grasshopper (Numbers 13:17-33). So the unknown held both promise and foreboding. It was wonderful and frightening at the same time. But in the end, the fear of the unknown was finally conquered by the conviction that the land could be—*must* be—entered into.

Fruit and giants—they're part and parcel of the unknown. The fruit of leaving sexual sin is a new and better way of living. But the giants scowl in the background. Loneliness, sexual temptation, misunderstanding from friends, and uncertainty about the future all loom large enough to make you chirp away like a grasshopper. The question is this: Are you going to cling to familiar, destructive ways simply because you can relate to them, or are you willing to abandon them in favor of a new way of living which is better, even though at this point you can't relate to it?

I trust that you're ready and willing to try something better, which means that you're ready and willing to repent.

Practical Repentance

For a practical model for repentance look at 2 Chronicles 15. In this account of revival in Israel, King Asa received a message from the prophet Azariah encouraging him to turn his backslidden subjects' hearts back toward the true God. Israel had been without a true priest for some time, and the nation was suffering spiritually without good leadership. Idolatry had become entrenched, and immorality had left the Israelites weakened and restless. King Asa was promised, however, that if he would sincerely seek God his land would be restored.

> When Asa heard these words...he took courage, and removed the abominable idols from all the land of Judah....Then he gathered all Judah and Benjamin, and those who dwelt with them. ...Then they entered into a covenant to seek the LORD God of their fathers with all their heart and with all their soul (2 Chronicles 15:8,9,12).

Asa responded to the call to repentance in three ways: He took courage, he took sweeping action, and he put everyone on notice that he had made a major decision that would affect all of his people.

1. *Asa took courage.* He needed it! Instituting a national revival was no small undertaking, and it was sure to be met with resistance and misunderstanding. "Why shake everything up?" some of the people no doubt moaned. "We've gotten comfortable with our idols and lifestyle." It required effort and fortitude on Asa's part to stick to his commitment. But he drew courage.

Courage is not an absence of fear; instead, it is a willingness to *do the very thing you are afraid of.* In this case, that willingness comes because you know that you have a divine mandate to repent, just as surely as Asa did. Courage didn't come to him because he knew everyone would applaud his actions. Instead, it came because he knew what he was proposing to do was right. That is your comfort, your source of courage: the knowledge that what you are doing is *right*, and the confident peace that comes with that knowledge.

2. *Asa took sweeping action.* All the idols in Judah and Benjamin were torn down and put away. They weren't stored away for safekeeping or covered up and hidden. They were put away.

You may never have categorized your sexual sins as "idolatry" because you haven't consciously worshiped them as one would worship an idol. But idolatry need not include literal worship. To commit idolatry you need only consider a person, activity, or thing to be more important than God. If you allow yourself to habitually indulge in anything that offends God, you are in essence saying that your pleasure is more important than His will. The difficulty of giving something up may cause you such stress and discomfort that you may decide it isn't worth putting yourself through the pain of withdrawal. Sometimes that's the price of righteousness—one which you may consider to be too high. In that case, not only has your sin become an idol, but your *self* has become one as well.

Some people, perhaps you, are literally addicted to sexual activities, and repenting of these activities is no small thing. There *is* such a thing as sexual bondage, or sexual addiction, if you will. I have seen it a number of times, and I'm grateful that this problem in our culture is finally getting the attention it deserves. To be sexually addicted is to literally rely on sex to stabilize you. It's a state in which the rush of sexual pleasure, with all its accompanying chemical forces, has become to you what a drug has become to an addict. And like a drug, it begins to interfere with all parts of life. Breaking the cycle of sexual addiction is not just a matter of will in this case; it's a matter of *strategy, consistency,* and *patience.* For some people it's a long, exhausting process.

But *repentance* begins that process. Without it there can be no growth, no freedom, no change. And repentance is an act of the will. So the ball is still in your court. Though breaking the patterns of sexual addiction is not *only* an act of the will, it certainly *begins* with an act of the will. (Further strategies for dealing with sexual addiction are mentioned in chapter 7, "Maintaining Sexual Integrity.")

To put away sexual idolatry, you first need to call it what it is: a form of sexual expression that has come between you and God, one which you are putting away once and for all in response to His command: "You shall have no other gods before Me." This creates a new frame of mind, a commitment to stop both the sexual acts and any activities that draw you toward them. It is, as I mentioned earlier, your anger, fear, or sense of futility which will sustain this commitment. All three can be valuable. Anger at the notion of anything controlling you keeps you from coming under its control again. Fear of ultimate consequences—disease, arrest, bondage—gives you the common sense to avoid anything that would draw you back into immorality. And a sense of the futility of sexual sin makes you loath to invest any more time and energy in it. In other words, repentance is evidenced by a changed attitude which expresses itself in concrete actions. You stop the activity and commit yourself to abstaining from it in the future.

3. *Asa put people on notice.* King Asa didn't go sneaking out at night in disguise, tearing down the idols while nobody was looking, and saying, "Shhh! I don't want to offend anyone!" The sins that had been openly committed had to be openly abandoned. This is an important principle too often

overlooked by repentant believers. When your particular sin involves other people (as homosexuality usually does), then those same people need to know you have abandoned that sin.

There are practical reasons for this. No matter how sincere you are, you're going to be tempted. That is a reality for all of us. When we're accustomed to getting satisfaction out of something, even when we've decided to give it up, we're drawn back toward it when times get rough.

Ever try dieting? If you have, you know that when you're depressed or frustrated you're especially prone to break your diet. Let's say you're used to eating out with some friends once a week at a pizza parlor. If they don't know you're dieting, won't they expect you to join them in some pizza during your next get-together? And if you're already feeling like breaking your diet anyway, won't it be easier to do so if no one knows you're trying to abstain from pizza?

Granted, there's a major difference between dieting and sex, but the same principle applies: When you abandon sexual sin, you will find yourself drawn back toward it at some point when you're feeling low. If the people you have been sexually active with don't know about your decision, it will make it that much easier for you to go back to your old patterns of behavior with them.

If you have been involved only in anonymous encounters, you can't very well track your partners down and make an announcement to them. There's no need to, anyway. Likewise, if your expression of homosexuality has been exclusively through fantasies or pornography, there really isn't another person to discuss this with. But if there are people you have been sexually involved with that you're still interacting with, they need to know about your decision. If you don't advise them of it now, you will just set yourself up for problems later on.

Case in Point: Brad

Brad entered counseling after a recent breakup with his lover. He had gotten into the relationship as a backslidden Christian, and after rededicating himself to the faith, he decided to finally deal with his homosexuality. But two stumbling blocks kept holding him back, both of which he could have avoided if he had only put people on notice. He was still strongly attracted to his ex-lover Jake, and none of his gay friends knew about his decision to give up homosexual activity. As a result, both his friends and his ex-lover expected him to go about his business as usual.

Brad still saw Jake on occasion. Each time he did, he was determined not to have sex with him, but Jake still expected a sexual encounter to cap off their time together, since he had no reason to believe that Brad would object. In spite of his best intentions, once they were alone together, Brad couldn't say no. Jake had expectations, Brad had attractions, and the inevitable happened time and again. Finally, instead of relying on sheer willpower, Brad confessed to Jake that he no longer felt homosexuality was an option for him. To his credit, Jake respected Brad's decision, though he disagreed with it, and they decided to keep their relationship nonsexual.

Dealing with his other gay friends was another matter. Brad wanted to avoid being "preachy," but he felt he was being dishonest with them by keeping his decision to himself. They in turn kept trying to play "matchmaker" with him by setting him up with new dates. The situation was getting pretty awkward, to say the least.

We worked out a simple way for Brad to discuss the problem with his friends. Since he had no intention of forcing his beliefs on them, Brad decided to tell them, one at a time, that he had come to view homosexual relationships as being incompatible with his faith. He asked each of them if they could continue their friendship with that understanding. Some gladly complied, while others took real offense to Brad questioning the validity of homosexuality. But at least the conflict was settled. Brad kept the friendships of those who could respect his right to live as he saw fit, and he continued to show them the same respect.

Some people would consider it wrong to maintain relations of any kind with gay friends or ex-lovers, but there is no hard-and-fast rule saying you should simply cut off those who disagree with you. The acid test is always this: If you can maintain a relationship that doesn't compromise your own beliefs, then do so. Discuss your differences, by all means, and be honest about where you stand. Then you can decide which relationships you can maintain, and which ones you will have to withdraw from.

By now your dissatisfaction with homosexuality should have crystallized into a motivation to change, and your motivation will have led you to take repentant action. You have identified what specifically you have needed to turn from, and you have turned from it and let the appropriate people know about your decision. Your repentance should be manifested by a change in behavior and outlook.

When John the Baptist called the people to repentance, he wasn't just asking for a decision. "Bear fruits worthy of repentance," he exhorted, meaning that tangible evidence always follows a true conversion. For now, the fact that you have turned away from old patterns is a part of that evidence. The next step, turning toward something new, begins when you lay a new foundation for growth.

Afterthoughts on
Repentance

The weeks following my repentance were the darkest I had ever experienced.

Not at first, though. First I had to clean my act up, which was oddly exciting.

All my porn had to go, of course. I had videotapes and magazines to throw out, and I felt a little pathetic when I ran out of boxes to put them in, realizing how much money and time I had spent having sex with phantoms. I had my cable service turned off, cancelled my subscriptions to erotic publications, located another place to live in another city. Friends had to be notified—I told only my closest friends, hoping to keep a relationship with them, naive (again) as to how hard that would really be.

Then relocation, a new church, a different job—different everything, it seemed. And the dreaded AIDS test, which was brand-new and, at the time, required a four-week waiting period before getting results. I sweated it out, got the good "You're HIV negative" news, then with the energy of newness now spent, I settled into a routine.

Only then did it hit me that during the past six years I had ruined everything good I had been given: a fruitful ministry, a loving family, great potential—all wasted, radically screwed up in a public, shameful way. I began visualizing the people I had preached to, baptized, and prayed with, hearing the news back in 1978 and responding to it: *Did you hear about Joe Dallas? Can you believe what he did?* I saw their faces, disappointed and disgusted with me. And I, in turn, sank into a bottomless disgust with myself.

Repentance wasn't joyful. It actually preceded the first time in my life I had ever been suicidal. I began sleeping through the days, then waking up horrified at myself, rehearsing again and again what I had done, each time seeing it in a worse light. Hundreds of sex partners, thousands spent on hookers, broken relationships, gross stupidity. I would cry, thrashing around in my bed, pondering suicide ("If I ask God's forgiveness *after* I take the pills but *before* I die, can I still get into heaven?"), hitting the walls with my fists and head, then going back into fits of weeping and moaning.

As part of my "penance," I called everyone I could locate from my days in the ministry to apologize and tell them I had repented. I could only find a few old friends, but one of them permanently interrupted the "I hate Joe" cycle I had gotten myself into.

When I got him on the phone and told him what was happening with me, the dam burst and I told him more than I had intended to: my guilt, the miserable state I was in, my fear that there was no life or future for me.

"Well, Joe," he said, "if banging your head into the wall is going to bring people into the kingdom or build up the body of Christ, please keep doing it. But if it won't, don't you think all this energy you're putting into self-pity could be put into doing something useful, even redemptive, with what's left of your life?"

That shut me up.

"And," he continued, "who knows but that someday, after you get through all this, you might have learned something worth passing on?"

He worked in Christian publishing. Six years later, as we kept in touch and he watched my life take its course, he asked me if I would be interested in writing a book, and *Desires in Conflict* was born.

So. What do you know?

Four

Laying the Foundation

*Remember the Biblical warning that faith without
deeds is of no value. Without purposeful action,
you're just a passenger, being pulled along without
self-imposed direction or control. Some people prefer
the passenger role. If you are one of those people,
you either need to wake up and take the controls,
or prepare to become one of life's crash test dummies—
and I emphasize DUMMIES.*

—FROM *LIFE STRATEGIES* BY PHILLIP ("DR. PHIL") MCGRAW

God never intended man to repent of sin for repentance's
sake alone. The higher purpose has always been to bring us
into a better life. Sin is abhorrent to God because it keeps
us from that better life. Without those "better things" to strive
for, what's the point in repentance?

Apply this truth to homosexuality and you will get a
clearer picture of God's intentions toward you. You're not
called to give up homosexuality just because it's "bad"; you
are invited to a life of wholeness which you cannot attain as
long as you hold on to anything that is second-best. Attaining
wholeness, though, means growth. And growth cannot come

until the things stifling it are abandoned. Repentance of homosexual behavior is just a means to an end, that end being the sexual and emotional health that is your spiritual birthright. That is what you and God are fighting for.

Growth requires a solid foundation—a lifestyle built on principles and actions that allow your growth to flourish. Your task at this point is to lay a foundation that is flexible enough to allow growth and strong enough to fall back on when you are tested. Believe me, if you don't have a foundation good enough to fall back on, you will just fall, period.

Houses depend on foundations made of concrete elements, sturdy enough to uphold the building during storms and earthquakes, strong enough to handle additions to the structure. The building process starts with the foundation, and everything that is built afterward stands or falls on that foundation's strength. So it had better be well-planned.

Personal growth is rooted in a solid foundation as well. To build it, you need to establish a lifestyle which regularly strengthens you. That is the best defense I know of against regression or backsliding. It is also the best way I know of to promote progress. Neglect your foundation or lay it without forethought, and you set yourself up for failure.

A good foundation is a lifestyle that pays regular attention to the following: spiritual disciplines, church fellowship, emotional support through specialized care, and social resources. These four elements provide the structure vital to true change. With structure there can be growth and expansion; without it there is only chaos.

Spiritual Disciplines

The essence of your strength lies in your spiritual health, and the essence of true spirituality is an intimate knowledge of God. Without this, Christianity is reduced to ritualistic dryness. You cannot hope to be fulfilled by going through the motions of service toward a God you feel far away from. Now, more than ever, you need to draw near.

Though this is true of all Christians, it's doubly true of you. You're dealing with a tough issue while making major life changes. For you to even attempt this without a solid spiritual base is as foolish as a man attempting to become a championship bodybuilder without the use of his arms. He's not going to pump much iron without those limbs, and you're not going to grow much without spiritual strength.

Spiritual strength comes through routine. Legalistic as that may sound, it's the people who incorporate prayer and Bible study into their day-to-day lives that exhibit the most success. That's because we cannot know God without investing time in communication with Him. That's applicable to all relationships, isn't it? We can't say we know someone if we haven't spent time talking to him, listening to him, experiencing closeness with him. And we certainly can't say we love someone whom we haven't taken the time to know.

There are plenty of people we interact with daily whom we don't really know because we invest no personal time in them. Look at your coworkers, for example. Chances are you spend a good deal of time in their company without knowing their real thoughts or feelings. You're together, but uninvolved. Sadly, we're prone to treat God like a coworker. We acknowledge His presence but invest no energy in personal communion with Him. We don't know Him, so how can we love Him?

The spiritual discipline of daily prayer and study of God's Word goes a long way toward correcting the problem. Incorporate it into your life now.

While doing so, avoid the tendency to take on more than you can handle. People who reestablish their spiritual disciplines are prone to unrealistic zeal, promising themselves and God that they will spend an hour in daily prayer after reading ten chapters of the Bible. Of course they give up after a few days, going back to no prayer life or study of the Word at all. You are not a cloistered monk, I assume, so don't try to act like one. Instead, start by setting aside at least 15 minutes daily for reading one chapter of the Bible and praying afterward. You can handle 15 minutes—I don't care what your schedule is like. And if you will make that a part of your daily routine—no excuses, no sloughing off—you will see changes quickly in all parts of your life.

Why the importance of both prayer and Bible reading? Because they are the two primary tools we use to know God. We listen to Him through His Word, and we speak to Him in prayer.

We are built up in faith by exposure to the Word (Romans 10:17), which cleanses us (John 15:3) and by which we are instructed in righteousness (Psalm 119:9). We communicate our needs through prayer, given the promise that our requests are heard when made according to His will (1 John 5:14,15). Those are general principles applicable to any believer.

There are other reasons you should be diligent in private devotions. Look at the changes you're making. Look at the struggles you're up against. Look at the number of people on one side who don't understand those struggles, then look at the number of people on the other side who think you shouldn't even try to change. Where are you going to find your strength and solace in the middle of all this, if not from God? And how will you ever find that solace in God if you're not willing to invest time and effort in cultivating your relationship with Him?

Another crucial point: How can you ever really know God's thoughts toward you without knowing Him personally? Do you realize that your attitude toward God has everything to do with the attitude you think He has toward you?

Men struggling with their sexuality often begin their process feeling alienated from God. They say they feel that way because of something they have done, usually something sexual that they were especially ashamed of. Further examination, though, shows that they felt that way long before they got involved in sexual sin. The sense of alienation from God really started when they began feeling alienated from people in general, especially important authority figures. To them, those figures represent God. That's pretty normal. Jesus used earthly fathers as models of God when He taught, because the illustration of a loving father would help people understand God's attitude toward them.

But what if the earthly father was perceived as unloving, impatient, distant? The heavenly Father will be perceived the same way. So a frustrating cycle begins: God is perceived as unloving because other authority figures seem to be unloving. That misconception can only be corrected by getting to know Him as He truly is.

If you are like most of us, you probably need a better understanding of God and His feelings about you. The wrong perception *of* Him creates the wrong response *to* Him. That can only be corrected by taking the time to know Him through private communicating. Make that a priority.

Church Fellowship

Church fellowship is as crucial to your foundation as private devotions. Hopefully you are already committed to a local church body. But I know there's a good chance you're not, because many people in your situation avoid the church.

The reasons vary. The one I hear most frequently is that the church doesn't understand the needs of people dealing with difficult life issues (quite true, sometimes). Therefore, they reason, church fellowship won't be of any benefit (quite false, always).

Remember, there are plenty of issues besides yours which most Christians don't understand, and plenty of other issues being mishandled by the church. But the benefit of fellowship isn't derived from being perfectly understood. It's derived from the encouragement and love expressed between believers. That love may be imperfect and the encouragement incomplete, but you can't grow without it. As long as there is a body of Christ, and as long as you're a part of it, you will need its other members.

Anger with Christians is another reason that many people give for shying away from fellowship. To a point that's understandable. Many Christians (though by no means *all* of them) have treated people like you pretty badly. To hear some of them talk, you would think homosexuality was the worst of all sins, the ultimate abomination (yet gossip, pride, and injustice are also cited as abominations in the Bible). And some believers hold such curious notions about homosexuality! Some people think you simply chose to have these desires. Others think you're not really a Christian if you have such feelings. And some would avoid you if they knew about your struggles, as though homosexuality was somehow contagious. So your anger is understandable, maybe even justifiable, to some degree.

But then again, you're in good company. The apostle Paul wasn't much of a saint in his early days. In fact, he was an aggressive, fanatical zealot dedicated to the eradication of Christianity. His zeal took on murderous proportions. He gave an approving nod to the murderers of Stephen, the first Christian martyr, even holding their cloaks for them while they stoned the young man to death. Paul—or Saul as he was known then—sought Christians out, dragging them before the religious authorities to have them charged, jailed, and executed. In fact, when he was apprehended by Christ on the road to Damascus, he was in the process of carrying out his violent mission.

Men like that normally develop a bit of a reputation. Is it any wonder that when he became a convert to Christianity other believers were reluctant to accept him into fellowship? Who could relate to his crimes? Who could be sure that he was sincere? And who wouldn't have just a touch of morbid curiosity about Paul's bloody past?

Like you, Paul was deeply misunderstood. His background haunted him, seeming to close the door on future relationships within the church. In fact, according to Acts 9:26, when he tried to join the believers in Jerusalem, they were afraid of him and doubted his authenticity as a disciple. He could have given up. He could have, with some justification, stomped his foot and said, "Hey, you guys were all sinners just like me, even though we all didn't commit the same sin! Why can't you just accept me as I am? You're not playing fair; I'm outta here!" Of course, to his credit and our benefit, he stuck it out.

And, as He always does, God provided Paul with a way out in the form of an understanding soul named Barnabas. Barnabas took a stand for Paul, convincing the other disciples that his conversion was genuine and his intentions good. He extended to Paul the right hand of fellowship, which bridged the gap between Paul and the Christians he had been alienated from.

Don't underestimate the entire body of Christ just because of painful experiences you have had with some Christians. Barnabas wasn't the first and last of his kind; there are other people who have been cut from the same mold. They often don't stand out, and they may be overshadowed by their less-sensitive brethren. But they exist, and if you refuse to give yourself a chance to encounter them, you'll miss one of Christianity's greatest joys—hearty fellowship—as well as one of the most important sources of healing.

Which brings us to the reason that you especially need to participate in a local church body. Homosexuality is a relational problem. It's characterized by a perverse form of sexual relating and has its origins in some sort of relational difficulties. I am convinced that healthy, intimate relationships are the key toward outgrowing homosexuality. And those relationships are best found among believers. It is the *church* which becomes your prime resource for relationships that build you up, encourage you, and promote your healing. Shun the church and you shun your own healing.

If you're not already in one, it's up to you to seek out a church. Thank God, we're in a nation rich in churches, which means you probably have several in your area to choose from. Naturally, yours needs to be one that upholds the authority of God's Word, preaches biblical Christianity, and encourages spiritual growth. Give yourself no excuses for putting this off. Fellowship is not optional; it's a basic part of the structure for your growth.

Specialized Care

Now is a good time to look into specialized help from people who have had experience dealing with homosexuality. That kind of help is usually available through professional counseling or specialized ministry, both of which are valuable and should be considered.

Although I include this as one of the four basic parts of a good structure, I should also say that you will, with or without specialized care, continue to grow. Your growth is a process involving you, God, and significant relationships. Professional help or specialized ministry helps the process along, to be sure, but it isn't the process itself. In other words, if such help isn't available, you are still capable of attaining your goals. But if such help is available, why shouldn't you take advantage of it?

Without hesitation, I suggest finding a Christian counselor. You shouldn't feel afraid of professional therapy, though you should approach it carefully. Author and cult expert Dave Hunt, an outspoken critic of most modern psychology, makes a good point when he allows that at times professional counseling can be helpful:

> We are not denying the value of professional counsel for those areas of daily function that are not covered in the Bible and do not find resolution solely through our relationship with God in Christ. In seeking counsel, however, it should always be biblical to the extent that the Bible covers the situation.[1]

There are many qualified Christian therapists who can help you identify conflicts and offer proper, godly counsel. It will be to your benefit to look into this. In a professional therapeutic environment you have the freedom to discuss things best left unsaid in other relationships. Your self-perception, fantasy life, sexual urges, and irrational moods can be explored without fear of social repercussion, with a person who is trained to take that information and correctly analyze it and offer suggestions that are unique to your situation. It gives you an opportunity to know yourself and to understand the roots of your behavior and desires. That alleviates anxiety, which is healing in itself, and it gives you useful information.

Sometimes looking for a therapist can be stressful enough to make you need one. It's hard to know who's best for you, and there is no guarantee, once you've started, that you have found the right one. But there are safeguards you can take to make the search easier.

Get a recommendation, if possible, from your pastor or a trusted Christian leader. That's always better than picking a name out of the directory. (Also see the Resources section in the back of this book for referrals to organizations that can connect you with a Christian counselor or a local ministry for support and counsel.) Find out before your first visit what the therapist's licensing or educational credentials are, and how much it will cost. Be specific about your needs; if possible, discuss them with the therapist over the phone before coming in. Tell him what you're dealing with and why you're looking for help.

Ask questions. Find out where he stands on homosexuality and Christianity, and specifically how he deals with these issues in therapy. Ask about his prior experience. Has he dealt with this before? How often? What kinds of results does he expect when doing therapy with someone in your position?

Don't feel you need to pick the first counselor you meet. It may be wise to visit a few counselors before making a decision to begin therapy. It's a major investment of finances and time, so consider it carefully.

Be sure you feel reasonably comfortable with a therapist before you commit yourself to working with him. "Reasonably comfortable" is a subjective term, I know, and therapy is never comfortable in the beginning anyway. But you should feel as though you're working with someone who knows what he's doing, is respectful of you and your feelings, and displays a genial, professional manner.

You should also consider the finances involved. You will be in counseling for a while, so review your budget, check your medical insurance to see if it covers mental health care, and plan accordingly.

I don't believe professional therapy is your only option, nor do I believe that you can't grow and change without it. But if it's feasible economically and good help is available, I urge you to take advantage of it.

Specialized Ministry

Another option is finding a specialized ministry to Christians dealing with homosexuality. If you don't know of any such ministries in your area, contact Restored Hope Network (listed in the back of this book in the Resources section) or check with your pastor. These ministries usually function as groups, combining prayer, teaching, and support. Joining up with such a group can alleviate the sense of isolation so common to the homosexual struggle and can provide real encouragement from other men who face many of the same issues that you do.

The insight you can gain from these groups is especially valuable. You can learn how other men handle sexual temptation or alleviate loneliness. And you get the benefit of learning from the mistakes of others.

You also learn acceptance of the things you cannot change. That's especially helpful, because often there's a period of frustration in the early stages of growth. Change becomes an obsession ("When will I feel differently toward my own sex and the opposite sex?") and patience wears thin. By meeting with people who share your struggles, you will see how they deal with homosexuality. You will get a better perspective, realizing that although you can't wish the presence of homosexuality away, you can diffuse the anxiety you feel over it.

Be careful though not to make a specialized support group your only social outlet. For a time it may be the one place you know of where you can meet people and feel comfortable, but that should be a temporary rather than a long-term situation. Never substitute specialized ministries for the local church body, and never limit your relationships to other support-group members. That will only deepen the feeling that you're different from everyone else, making you feel as though only another "struggler" can relate to you. That leads to narrow friendships, based primarily on a mutual wound, in which the topic of discussion is usually homosexuality and healing. That's unhealthy, and boring as well. Who wants to talk about *this* all the time?

A specialized ministry should, among other things, teach you better ways of relating so you can establish other friendships outside the group. It's a bridge toward more social integration—a place to heal wounds, gather strength, and move on.

Social Alliances

Your resources should include at least one intimate friend (preferably more than one) and some acquaintances.

Intimate friends provide your main source of support. You confide in them and rely on their input to stabilize you. They make you feel important. They prove to you that you are significant, unique, worthwhile. Sometimes their love for you is the one thing that keeps you from despair.

Acquaintances are sometimes looked on as second-rate friendships ("He's not a *friend*, just an *acquaintance*."), but they are valuable in their own right. They offer variety and fun. Your interactions with them color your life and broaden your perspective. When you go to parties you see them, lightly interact, and feel refreshed. That, too, is vital to emotional health.

Social resources—friends and acquaintances—are terribly overlooked and underrated as prime agents of healing. Often when I ask a new counselee what sort of social life he has, he blinks and says, "What's that got to do with homosexuality?"

Plenty. Relationships are your most valuable resources. You've got to know that you are significant to somebody else, appreciated for your gifts and uniqueness. And you've got to know that you have people to lean on, people interested in your life and rooting for you as you grow.

Your relationship with your therapist, pastor, and support-group members will offer you some of those benefits. But you need more. You need to know that you are valued for your total self, not just because you have a problem requiring special care. And that knowledge will come only through friendships. They form a vital part of your foundation.

So take stock. Whom are you close to right now as you read this? What friendships do you have that are deep, have some longevity to them, and are dependable? Your close friends are your allies, and allies are crucial. If you have them, nurture them. A good foundation will include regular, planned contact with intimate friends.

Take stock of your acquaintances as well. Keep in touch with them and follow up on those "Let's have lunch" promises. Time spent with acquaintances is relaxing, energizing time. It shouldn't be a rarity. Make it part of your lifestyle.

I'm harping on this friendship/acquaintance concept because I've noticed that counselees who socialize make quicker progress, are less prone to depression, and keep a better attitude. Their contacts keep them buoyant, even when they're dealing with painful emotional issues. Most important, I think, is the effect that friendship has on their self-perception. It literally corrects the false concepts they have grown up with ("I'm different than everyone else. I don't have anything to offer."), proving them to be wrong and changing the way the counselee responds to people in general. That's just the sort of change you need.

If you don't have social resources, you're at a real disadvantage. I urge you to take this to heart: Without friendships you are incomplete. If you have them, strengthen them. If you don't have them, do whatever is necessary to make them. (Chapter 8 will cover some strategies for social integration.)

Foundation-laying requires time management. You need to plan time for devotions, church attendance, social activities. If you need some help with basic time management and prioritizing, Gordon MacDonald's book *Ordering Your Private World* (Thomas Nelson Publishers) will be of real use to you. It cuts through the excuses we give for poor planning and gives clear, workable solutions for the confusion of a disorganized private life. While you're at it, if you don't have an appointment book, pick one up. Plan your weeks in advance, blocking out regular time for laying and strengthening your foundation. You may be surprised how much time is really available when it's mapped out beforehand.

Your foundation undergirds your process. It contains the resources that hold you up while you struggle toward growth, so it had better be solid. Once it's laid, though, it requires tending. That's what makes this foundation less like concrete and more like a garden. It needs to be watched and cared for regularly. Any of its elements will decay if they're neglected. So your foundation, like a chain, is only as strong as its weakest point.

Build it carefully; watch it constantly.

Afterthoughts on
Laying the Foundation

This is a structure plan I work out with my clients. Please try it—I think it will provide a simple, workable recovery plan you can begin incorporating now.

First, take some lined paper and jot these questions down, giving yourself ample space after each question to answer it fully:

1. What event or circumstances motivated your decision to repent of homosexuality?

2. What specifically will you need to repent of (turn from)? (Examples: use of pornography, ongoing relationship, anonymous sexual encounters, Internet porn, phone sex, etc. Be specific and honest.)

3. List any ways your sexual behavior has affected you physically.

4. List any ways your sexual behavior has affected you mentally or emotionally. (Examples: mental images, depression, loss of self-respect, fear, distraction.)

5. List any ways your sexual behavior has affected you spiritually. (Examples: loss of intimacy with

God, spiritual attack, withdrawal from fellowship.)

6. Describe what your life will be like five years from now if you *don't* stop this behavior. (Include a description of how this behavior will affect your marriage, job, spiritual life, relationships, and view of yourself.)

7. You just described what your life will be like if you continue in this behavior. Is this acceptable to you? Why or why not?

Second, if you don't have a regular devotional life, begin *now* by naming a book of the Bible you can begin reading *today*.

Book: _____

Beginning with chapter: _____

If you haven't read the Bible before, or if you've been out of the habit for a while, let me suggest the following books to read in this order, to get you started:

1. Gospel of John

2. Epistle to the Romans

3. Epistle to the Ephesians

4. Epistle from James

5. Proverbs

Begin reading a chapter from the books just listed for ten minutes each day, followed by five minutes of prayer, followed by this verbal recommitment: "For the next 24 hours I recommit myself to sexual purity."

Next, begin a motivation review journal by using the following page and listing ten reasons for staying sexually pure. (I have given you five examples to start you off; just list ten more.) Then list five more every week for the next four weeks. You will then have 35 reasons for staying pure. Review them daily. You will find that at least a few of these will motivate you on any given day.

Motivation Review Journal

1. I want intimacy with God.

2. I want to become the sort of man I can honestly respect.

3. I'm tired of lying, hiding, and covering up.

4. I want peace of mind.

5. I don't want to be a part of the world's problem(s).

Now either write down the six-item plan listed on the next page, or tear this page out of the book and keep it posted where you can refer to it. This is a basic set of disciplines you need to add to your routine *now*. Think of it the way you would think of a budget or a diet: Keep it *simple*, keep to it *daily*, and keep verifying *week to week* that you're staying with it.

You'll notice it adds a total of 20 minutes to your daily schedule and approximately three hours to your weekly schedule.

Prayer and Scripture	15 minutes daily
Motivation review	5 minutes daily
Support group	90 minutes weekly

(Contact the Restored Hope Network web site listed in the Resources section of this book for a ministry in your area.)

Recreation   2 hours twice monthly
(Plan something enjoyable and entertaining, preferably with friends, at least twice a month for a minimum of two hours.)

Pastoral care   30 minutes monthly
(Ask for a half hour of your pastor's time once a month. It's crucial that you "check in" with him to update him on your progress, your difficulties, and to get any prayers/insight he may have to offer.)

Therapy   1 hour weekly
(Contact 1-800-NEW-LIFE, or the NARTH web site in the Resources section of this book, or contact Restored Hope Network for a referral.)

Structure is to you and me what insulin is to the diabetic. It's the medication we need daily to keep us on track. Take yourself off your medication, and you're sure to be overtaken. Structure, then, outdoes zeal and enlightenment in importance. I've come to believe, in fact, that without structure virtually nothing will be maintained, and no progress can be expected.

Five

Why Me?

Man is a stately castle, intricately and masterfully constructed. The castle, however, was given a life of its own. When man took it on himself to be God, he ruined everything—the decay became so extensive that only one with the eyes of a craftsman could see the structural beauty that remained underneath. Man is an amalgamation of dignity and depravity, a glorious ruin.

—FROM *THE WOUNDED HEART* BY DAN ALLENDER

So far we have concentrated on decision-making and integrity because they lay the foundation that makes growth possible. This is a principle repeated throughout Scripture: God calls a person or a people to obedience, giving them some basic promises, then waits until they have responded in obedience before revealing more truth.

The children of Israel were told they would be delivered from bondage and brought into a new home. Only after their departure from Egypt (obedience) did God reveal more of Himself through the law and divine guidance. Christ's disciples followed a similar pattern: They were called, they responded, they were taught. And Paul, after his conversion, was given bits and pieces of guidance. Only after obeying God's initial commands did he come into deeper revelations.

Remember: The *how* is always more important than the *why*. Learning *how* to abstain from my sin is crucial; learning *why* my particular sin ever developed is *helpful*, but *optional*.

So it was necessary for you as well to respond first through conformity to God's standards. You repented of homosexual sin (if you were involved in any), then laid a foundation for growth. Now you can enter into a stage of enlightenment. It's time to learn about yourself—to learn what lies behind your homosexual attractions, why they exist, and how they have affected your ability to relate to yourself and other people.

We're going to look at some theories on the origins of the homosexual orientation. In so doing, we will try to answer a fundamental question you have asked yourself hundreds of times: Why me?

Why you, indeed? You never asked for homosexual attractions. You never decided to incorporate them into your sexual makeup. Given the choice, you might have picked any number of problems before choosing this one. As for the conflicts creating your homosexuality, we know you didn't choose those, either. You didn't decide what family you would be born into, you didn't choose to respond to early events in a given way, and you certainly didn't have anything to say about those responses when they became sexual. You are in many ways a victim of circumstance. As far as the development of your attractions to the same sex is concerned, you're blameless. God does not and will not hold that against you. It is not a sin to be homosexually inclined. It's what you *do* with those inclinations that condemns or commends you.

With that in mind, we will look to two sources to help us understand where it all began: the past, and developmental theories having to do with homosexuality.

Learning from Our Past

Many Christians are reluctant to study their past. After all, "the past" has traditionally been the great scapegoat. "I can't help doing the things I do because such and such happened to me. I'm not really responsible," or so goes the message that many self-analyzed subjects would have us believe. That just isn't true, and that sort of blame-placing should be avoided at all costs. The past, no matter how difficult, doesn't force us to behave in certain ways, and we can't duck our culpability in the present by blaming an unhappy childhood or a traumatic event. We alone are responsible for our actions; any philosophy which teaches otherwise should be avoided.

But a look at the past can help us understand our present condition and can give us useful information with which we can correct our present problems. We can learn from the past and thus improve the present.

Scripture has something to say about this. Much of the Old Testament consists of explanations gleaned from history which help us understand the present. The fall of man, the formation of the Hebrew people, and the victories and failures of the patriarchs are all detailed in the Old Testament. Paul succinctly describes the value of learning about these and other past events by telling us that "all these things happened to them as examples, and they were written for our admonition" (1 Corinthians 10:11). In short, the past helps us to understand the present. And what we understand, we can deal with.

Psychology is another area of controversy among Christians. It needn't be, because the study of human behavior is worthwhile. The book of Proverbs is full of psychological thought, so God clearly commends it when properly used. The fact that much of today's psychology is polluted with anti-Christian teaching should not scare us away from the field itself. It should make us cautious, even skeptical at times, but not unwilling to examine what it has to offer that is of merit. There's nothing wrong with psychological theory per se, unless and until it usurps the authority of the Scriptures or becomes the end-all and be-all solution to human problems.

Here is a simple test to determine whether or not a psychological theory is valid: If it contradicts the Bible, reject it outright. It's false. If it's not spelled out in Scripture, but doesn't contradict it either, at least accept its possibility. It might be true. If it's in the Bible, affirm it as absolute truth. Within these guidelines we will consider some theories on homosexuality. Our goal here is knowledge because, as Solomon said, "A wise man is strong, yes, a man of knowledge increases strength" (Proverbs 24:5). Solomon commends learning as strength, and strength makes for a solid recovery.

Knowledge also reduces anxiety. Because of the stigma attached to homosexuality, strugglers often battle not only their attractions but also intense anxiety because of those attractions. This anxiety leads them to draw false conclusions about themselves that are damaging. They assume it's somehow all their fault. "I'm an unusually rotten person," they figure, "because only a rotten person would have a problem like this." But the more they learn about the nature of homosexuality, the more their anxiety fades. They feel less separated from the rest of humanity, because they realize their sexual desires indicate basic though unfulfilled needs—needs which are similar to everyone else's. The way they have been expressed may not have been normal, but the needs themselves are. It's a relief to learn that.

To better answer the question, Why me? we will look at some general theories on the origins of homosexuality, then compare them to the experiences of men who share your struggle.

Biological Theories

Biological theories deserve mention because they answer another question you have probably considered: Was I born this way?

It might seem so. You may remember feeling "different" from day one. Perhaps you even remember having homosexual fantasies at an early age. And if your struggle has been a long one, you may have wondered if its stubbornness is caused by biological ingredients.

It has been shown that there *may* be biological influences which could *predispose* a person toward homosexuality. The key word here is *predispose,* as in "having a tendency toward something." People can be born with predispositions toward any number of problems—depression or alcoholism, for example—yet that doesn't make the problems inevitable. It is the environment which brings predispositions to fruition.

"It is not for psychoanalysis to solve the problem of homosexuality," Freud said in his 1920 essays on sexuality. "It must rest content with discovering the psychical mechanisms that resulted in the determination of the object-choice. There its work ends, and it leaves the rest to biological research."

Whether or not they took their cues from Freud, scientists and sex researchers have certainly tried to discover a biological cause for homosexuality. Yet none has been found. There is no biological factor shown to be consistently present in homosexually oriented people. (See Appendix 1, The "Born Gay" Question, for a fuller treatment of the question of inborn homosexuality.)

Prenatal Influences

Research does show that there *may be* prenatal influences on the development of homosexuality in *some* cases, yet these

influences do not *determine* homosexuality. Background studies on the mothers of homosexual males, for example, showed
in some cases a history of marked stress during their preg-
nancies. Stress affects the hormone levels of expectant mothers and consequently the hormone levels in the child they
are carrying. Dr. John Money and associates at Johns Hopkins
University drew similar conclusions, citing the "Adam/Eve
principle" as an explanation for the effects of hormonal imbal-
ance on the unborn child's brain: "According to the Adam/
Eve principle, simply stated, if the fetal brain is not hormonalized, it will develop from its early sexually bipotential stage
to be, like Eve, feminine. To be like Adam, it must be
hormonalized."[1] For masculinity to emerge in the fetal brain,
Money theorizes, an adequate hormone level is necessary.
If that level is disrupted, the brain of a male child will become
"feminized" and have inborn feminine characteristics.

Likewise, researcher Gunter Dorner proposed in 1976
that male homosexuals may have developed a "feminine
sexual brain" caused by androgen deficiency, a conclusion he
based on a study of "effeminate" homosexual men.

Having said that, can we conclude hormonalization by
itself creates an inborn attraction to the same sex? Hardly.
Consider this sampling of professional remarks on the subject:

> The child's psychosexual identity is not writ-
> ten, unlearned, in the genetic code, the hormonal
> system or the nervous system at birth.[2]

> The genetic theory of homosexuality has been
> generally discarded today...no serious scientist
> suggests that a simple cause-effect relationship
> applies.[3]

> The idea that people are born into one type
> of sexual behavior is foolish.[4]

So we are now left facing the multitude of theories about the development of homosexuality. From Freud to the present, theorists have proposed that it can be traced to a dominant mother, a hostile father, an early sexual molestation, a fear of women, or any combination of the above.

My objection to all these theories is not that they are necessarily wrong, but that they assume each person has same-sex attractions for the same reason. I would argue that, like other problems, the roots of homosexuality vary from individual to individual.

It's wiser to approach this subject with a respect for the complexity of human sexuality in general. There is much we don't know about sexual preferences and behaviors—how they develop, why they arise in certain people but not in others. So we've got a lot to learn about homosexuality. We don't have all the answers, and I'm sure we never will.

Having said that, I will offer some thoughts on the development of homosexuality. And while I'm open to new theories on the subject and to the fact that no one can say for certain what causes this in all cases, I have seen a recurring pattern in case after case. Specifically, I've come to believe that homosexual attractions develop along these lines:

1. A child's perception of his or her relationship to parents or significant others.

2. A child's emotional response to those perceptions.

3. Emotional needs arising from these perceptions and responses.

4. The sexualization of those emotional needs.

This pattern allows for a number of childhood experiences, placing the emphasis not so much on what did or didn't happen but on the way the child perceived it. That explains the variety of childhood histories found among homosexually oriented adults. Some actually had wonderful parents, while some were raised by tyrants. It was their *perception* of their early relationships, not necessarily the facts themselves, that generated a response.

Consider a rather general example. A boy is raised by a father who adores him, spends time with him, and provides well for his family. Then, through circumstances beyond the father's control, he has to take a second job which keeps him away from the home. The boy is too young to understand economic realities; all he knows is that Dad is gone, and he takes that as a personal rejection. It doesn't matter whether or not his father has really rejected him. He *perceives* his father's absence as rejection and responds accordingly. He feels hurt, develops a resentment toward his father, and emotionally withdraws from the person he feels rejected by.

In another family, a boy is raised by a father who truly dislikes him. He makes no bones about it, telling his son that he wishes he had never been born and that he wants nothing to do with him. This child, too, feels hurt, develops a resentment toward his father, and emotionally withdraws from the person he feels rejected by.

Two children from completely different backgrounds, both responding to early pain in the same way. Both have experienced disruption in their relationship with the parent of the same sex, and both have responded emotionally to that disruption.

The response in each case will affect their relationships with their peers as well. They may feel insecure with others of their sex, assuming that because their parents rejected them, other people will do the same. Their identity—specifically their *gender* identity—might be shaken. Or they may retain a fantasy of having the perfect parent, an idealized parent they dream about and wish they could have as a parent or friend. Or they might simply feel unusually strong needs for bonding with the same sex, but because of their parent's perceived rejection, they avoid their peers to protect themselves from any further rejection.

As perception generates emotional response, so emotional response creates emotional needs. If these children suffer gender-identity disturbances, for example, they will keenly feel the need for a strong, accepting male to identify with. If they hold onto their fantasy of an ideal image, they will feel the need to find and bond with someone who matches that image. And if they feel alienated from peers of the same sex, they will feel especially strong needs for attention and approval from the very ones they feel alienated from.

Emotional needs can and do sometimes become sexualized. That is, at some point they are linked with sexual desires, so the object of the emotional need also becomes the object of sexual desire.

Because I believe this pattern to hold true in so many cases, I consider homosexuality to be a *function* through which *sexualized emotional needs* are fulfilled. This fulfillment may come through homosexual desires, or fantasies, or activities. The function is still the same.

Let me explain this further by examining each stage of this pattern.

Perception of Early Relationships

Most theorists agree that, whatever the cause of homosexuality, its development begins early, long before a child is able to actively choose or reject it. Since a child's parents are the most significant people in his life, his perception of them and of his relationship with them will profoundly influence his emotional development.

Your home was the first place you learned about relationships, and the lessons you learned there have influenced and still influence the way you relate to everyone. I'm sure that's why God places such importance on the family, setting it apart as sacred and vital. Within our homes we learn about marriage, friendship, brotherhood, and intimacy. We learn from what we see and experience, and we assume that what we are learning at home will hold true throughout life.

The family unit is also the first place you learned about yourself. You learned how valuable you were or were not from your family. You developed ideas about your "lovableness" from the responses you got at home. There you were taught, directly or indirectly, how important you, your feelings, and your opinions were and are.

That's because, as a child, you naturally assumed that your parents were godlike—all-powerful, all-wise, and always right. After all, they were the big people, the ones in charge, and you were the dependent, limited child. So what they thought of you, you came to think of yourself. Your identity has been learned with the help of people who taught you, through your interaction with them, about yourself. Identity is not something we just come into on our own. Outside influences shape our sense of who we are.

You can see this in the Genesis account of Creation. Adam didn't just wake up one day and decide, "Oh, I guess I'm the first created human. Nice garden I've got here; I think I'll keep the place up. And that lovely lady must be my wife, so I'll mate with her and we'll populate the planet." No, he learned who he was, what was expected of him, and how much he was worth from *God*. It was God who taught him his purpose in life, and it was God who, through constant care and provision, gave him a sense of identity.

Christians are also subject to this. When we're converted we begin to relearn our identity. Much of the Bible, especially the New Testament, teaches us who we are, why we are, and how important we are in God's sight. We, like Adam and the newborn child, learn our identity through another, higher source.

But we don't learn this exclusively through verbal teaching. It's not just our parents' *words* that we consider and take to heart; it's also their *responses* to us that teach us about ourselves. These are "messages"—nonverbal but clear communications between parent and child. They come in the form of a look, a touch, a tone of voice, even the amount of time they spend with us. Each of these sends us a message—not just about our parents but about ourselves. If a parent sends a child affirming messages through affection and attention, the child learns that he is safe and important because the parents say so. Likewise, when negative, hurtful messages are sent from parent to child, the child learns that he is not wanted, not valuable, unacceptable. Remember, the child has little confidence in his own insights, so he trusts his parents' judgment in these matters. "If Mom or Dad doesn't like me," he reasons, "then the problem is with me, not them. They know best; what they say goes." Remember, too, that the messages they send can be misinterpreted by the child.

An early perception of rejection or indifference from the parent of the same sex can be seen in the backgrounds of many homosexually oriented adults. In his book *Male Homosexuality,* Dr. Richard Friedman cites 13 independent studies from 1959 to 1981 on the early family lives of homosexuals. Out of these 13, all but one concluded that, in the early parent-child interactions of adult homosexuals, the subject's relationship with the parent of the same sex was unsatisfactory, ranging from a distant, nonintimate relationship to an outright hostile one. Most of the studies also indicated problems between the subjects and their parents of the opposite sex, but those problems were secondary in most cases.

These studies, by the way, were not conducted only with patients seeking professional help for their homosexuality. Studies by Evans (1969), Apperson and McAdoo (1968), Snortum (1969), Thompson (1973), Stephan (1973), Saghir and Robins (1973), and Bell, Weinberg, and Hammersmith (1981) were all performed with nonclinical subjects—people who were not undergoing psychotherapy and were not necessarily in distress over their homosexuality. Even these groups acknowledged that early in life something had gone wrong.[5]

Friedman, who does not approach the subject of homosexuality from a Christian perspective and is, in fact, highly sympathetic to the gay rights movement, concludes, "The weight of evidence discussed here seems therefore to implicate a pattern of family interactions in the development of homosexual men."[6] Later he reiterates the point by saying, "An emotionally secure, non-traumatic, warm and supportive pattern has not been documented to occur with any frequency in the backgrounds of homosexual men."[7]

As early as 1941, W.D. Fairbain presented similar ideas:

> Frustration of his desire to be loved and to have his love accepted is the greatest trauma that a child can experience. Where relationships with outer objects (i.e., parents) are unsatisfactory, we also encounter such phenomena as…homosexuality and [these] phenomena should be regarded as attempts to salvage natural emotional relationships which have broken down.[8]

Does this mean that a faulty relationship with parents creates homosexuality? Not necessarily. Many heterosexuals have come from families that were highly dysfunctional. Many boys have been raised by unloving and even cruel fathers whose mistreatment didn't cause their sons to turn to other men for sex. *Problems between parent and child do not necessarily cause homosexuality.* And yet the fact remains that these problems existed in the family backgrounds of most homosexually inclined adults. Why?

First, let's remember that sin manifests itself in any number of ways, yet sin is still the root problem. So a boy who is unloved by his father will develop some type of problem later in his life. Drugs, violent behavior, or antisocial tendencies might all be traced back to this root. Homosexuality is only one of many possible manifestations of poor family relationships.

But let me take this point even further. Perhaps it's not what *actually happened* between you and your parents that contributed to your homosexuality. Instead, it was the way you *perceived* your relationship with them and the way you emotionally *responded* to that perception. (This may explain why your sexual development took a different turn from your brother's or sister's. You responded in one way; they responded in another.)

Perception and *response* are the two key words here. In all relationships, we perceive the other party as having a certain attitude toward us, and we respond to the other party according to our own perception of their attitude. If we think somebody likes us, whether they really do or not, we will feel comfortable with him and probably want his friendship. Likewise, if we perceive someone else as being unfriendly and rejecting, we will tend to avoid him.

Haven't you seen this principle at work in your social life? Remember the times you have wanted to get to know someone, only to feel, because of the way he looked at you or because of his tone of voice, that he wanted nothing to do with you? No doubt you responded to your perception by saying, "Who needs him anyway?" or by feeling hurt and rejected. Later you may have found that you completely misunderstood him. You may have learned he was just in a bad mood when you met him, or that he's rather shy at first and doesn't warm up until he gets to know a person better. In those cases you found that your initial perception was wrong and that you had responded to a misconception.

Likewise in your early years you may have had parents who loved and highly valued you, but for some reason the communication of that love got blurred. You may have perceived your father to be disinterested in you, when in fact he cared very much about every part of your life. Still, you didn't respond emotionally to what really was—only to what you *thought* was reality.

In both cases, whether your same-sex parent actually rejected you or whether you simply perceived that rejection, you responded emotionally to what you saw or perceived. And that emotional response was probably the beginning of strong, unfulfilled needs, contributing to erotic same-sex attractions.

Emotional Responses to Early Perceptions

The response to an early perception of rejection may take three forms, all of which can contribute to homosexuality: problems of gender identity, an idealized image, or same-sex deficits.

1. *Problems of gender identity.* Your gender identity is your basic sense or perception of your masculinity or femininity. Money and Ehrhardt describe it as "the private experience of gender role, and gender role is the public expression of gender identity." Your gender role is the role your culture expects you to play as a man or woman, so of course it varies from culture to culture. Your gender identity is determined by your confidence in that role. Since our society places a

high premium on gender roles, your ability or inability to fulfill them seriously affects your general well-being.

Gender Identity Disorder is a clinical term describing a serious conflict between a person's *assigned* gender (male or female) and his *desired* gender. This disorder may show itself in transsexualism, or the desire of a man to actually be a woman, and vice versa. But Gender Identity Disorder is a far cry from homosexuality and is not commonly found among homosexually oriented adults.

But Dr. Friedman points out that feelings of being unmasculine or unfeminine are common among such adults. He proposes that unmasculinity, for example, is not necessarily femininity, but a lack of confidence in a boy's/man's own ability to fulfill the masculine role. This unmasculine or unfeminine experience, which I consider to be a *problem of gender identity* rather than a *Gender Identity Disorder*, has been noted by a number of investigators. Ten studies cited by Friedman, conducted between 1962 and 1984, have turned up the same results: a link between problems of gender identity and adult homosexuality (Friedman, 1988).

For example in 1981 Bell, Weinberg, and Hammersmith interviewed 979 homosexual men and 477 heterosexual men to determine which developmental ingredients may affect sexual orientation. Among their findings was evidence that "gender nonconformity" (their term) was closely linked to homosexuality:

> Even among non-effeminate homosexual men this Dislike of Boys Activities is the strongest predictor of Adult Homosexuality. While their nonconformity may not have been so obvious either when they were growing up or in adulthood, it would appear that where they thought they stood on a masculine-feminine continuum

when they were young was predictive of their eventual sexual orientation (Bell, Weinberg, and Hammersmith, *Sexual Preference: Its Development in Men and Women*, 1981).

How does this problem of gender identity come about? Like homosexuality, it is not inborn, but acquired through interactions, perceptions, and responses. A secure masculine or feminine identity usually develops through bonding with an older figure of the same sex, usually the father or mother, and emulating that older figure.

In the early 1980s, a delightful Australian film titled *The Bear* came out in American theaters. In it a young grizzly cub, orphaned after his parents were shot by hunters, tries to bond with an older grizzly, who at first wants nothing to do with him. But the cub shows remarkable tenacity, trying to snuggle up to the older bear whenever he sees him, only to be rebuffed and swatted away. Finally, when the older grizzly is shot by those same hunters, the young cub wins his heart by licking the gunshot wounds the grizzly is unable to reach. The two bond, and throughout the film the cub develops more "adult grizzly" characteristics by identifying with his surrogate father.

The film provides a pretty good model of gender identity development. When the father/mother figure is willing to bond with the child of the same sex, this invites the child to emulate and identify with the parent. The child will be inclined toward this process, desiring it intensely, but avoiding it if he feels unwelcome or unaccepted by the parent.

Should that avoidance occur, it can be the beginning of gender identity problems. As mentioned earlier, the child views the parent as "right"; that is, if the parent seems to reject the child, the child assumes it's his fault, not the parent's.

This can undermine a child's confidence not only as a person but also as a boy or girl. Problems of gender identity, then, begin with the child's belief that he is unacceptable to the parent of his sex, and therefore unacceptable to all members of his sex. This robs him of confidence to fulfill his gender role, having felt no invitation to emulate and identify with his father or she with her mother, leading to acute feelings of unmasculinity or unfemininity.

These feelings are confirmed during later development. After all, confidence with peers is largely determined by confidence at home. So if a boy feels ill-equipped to deal with other boys through traditional masculine activities, he will be inclined to avoid those activities, which disrupts his ability to bond with other boys, which reinforces his belief that he is unmasculine.

Case in Point—Gerard

Gerard remembers his earliest years as pleasant ones during which he related freely to both parents, though he felt mildly intimidated by his father, who was a machinist—rugged, tall, and noticeably masculine. One unfortunate incident triggered a series of events that would shape his sexual development. During a particularly heated argument with his mother that was taking place in Gerard's presence, his father picked him up and threw him across the room. While he cowered in the corner, the fight ensued for another hour or so, followed by a tense silence. When it was all over, the whole family gathered together and watched television as though nothing had happened. Gerard was five at the time and couldn't comprehend what had happened. Nor could he understand his father's silence—no apology, no explanation. He concluded (wrongly) that Dad disliked him. Gerard began to withdraw from the man, preferring the company of his mother, who seemed safer and more predictable.

His withdrawal didn't go unnoticed by his father, who apparently didn't understand Gerard's reasons for avoiding him. This only enraged him, causing him to resent what he perceived as Gerard's rejection of *him*. He began criticizing the boy, taunting him with labels like "sissy" and "Mommy's little girl." Gerard, of course, responded by retreating further from his father and assuming that he was indeed more acceptable to girls than to boys. With that perception of himself, he entered elementary school believing he should play with the girls, which reinforced his gender identity problems and caused other boys to likewise consider him a sissy. The label stuck (even though there was nothing noticeably feminine about Gerard), and he went through his first 23 years of life convinced he was decidedly unmasculine.

2. *Idealized image.* It's not uncommon for children to idealize their parents; in fact, it's uncommon for them not to. After all, Daddy looks pretty big and powerful to a little boy, and Mommy looks beautiful and competent to a little girl. Children naturally want to be like their same-sex parent, at least for a time. They see them as powerful, wise, and ideal.

Normal development allows for a gradual disappointment in our parents. If you're a parent you know that, sooner or later, you're going to blow it. You cannot possibly be the perfect mom or dad your kids want you to be. So eventually, to some degree, they will be disappointed in you just as, to some degree, you have been disappointed in your own parents.

That is actually good for us, because through disappointment we become more realistic and mature. We learn through this disappointment to accept people's limitations.

And so a child's ideal image of his father or mother gradually changes to a more realistic viewpoint. As he grows, he is able to see his parents' imperfections, but since he is growing emotionally as well as physically, he can handle the knowledge that they are not perfect. That is basic process: As we grow, biologically and emotionally, we learn to accept hard realities like death, injustice, and our parents' imperfections. The more we mature, the better able we are to let go of our early idealism.

At times, though, this process is aborted by early trauma. If a child is shocked by a sudden rejection from a parent or a parent's early disappearance, he might not have the capacity to handle the loss. Instead of gradually relinquishing the ideal image he had of his father, he may cling to it, hoping to someday find it again in somebody else.

Case in Point: Alan

Alan's early tragedy is a good example. He had seen little of his father during the first three years of his life. He and his sister were raised by his mother while his dad worked a graveyard shift. Alan vaguely remembers the few times he had been alone with Dad, times during which he felt Daddy was the most wonderful person in the world. He saw his father as a remote, godlike figure whom he could occasionally get a glimpse of. But unknown to him, his father was having severe episodes of depression and had been undergoing intensive therapy.

Shortly before his third birthday, Alan's father called him into the kitchen. He sat him down at the table, smiling strangely and saying, "Watch this." He then poured himself a glass of wine mixed with chemicals, gulped it down, and passed out. Within minutes, he died as Alan watched in confused horror.

The shock was too much for the three-year-old boy. Rather than face the full weight of what had happened, he retained the idealized image he had had of his father. It provided him with comfort during the following years, and throughout his life he looked for this image to show itself in other men. It finally did, in the form of a man who propositioned Alan and initiated his first homosexual encounter. Though he was well into his fifties at the time, his need for a wonderful man to take care of him expressed the longings of an unfulfilled child.

3. *Same-sex deficits.* There is a period of life, usually between early childhood and preadolescence, during which we almost exclusively seek out members of our own sex. Boys cluster with boys, and girls cling to each other. Sometimes kids express an almost-lighthearted contempt for each other. Little boys think girls are "weird"; the girls think the little boys have "cooties." That's normal, even necessary. Our identity as male or female is solidified when we bond with our own gender. Only when our need for bonding with the same sex has been fulfilled can we move on to relationships with the opposite sex.

During this period I believe there are three kinds of relationships with our own sex that we especially need: a nurturer, a mentor, and a comrade.

Our same-sex *nurturer* will usually be our parent of the same sex. This parent welcomes us to bond with him, making us feel comfortable and accepted in his presence. Our relationship with him is marked by physical affection, play, and intimate caring. He delights in us, giving us a sense of specialness. As we become secure in his love, we develop an early conviction that we're okay as males or females, perfectly acceptable and lovable to our same-sex nurturer and therefore to other members of our sex.

Our same-sex *mentor* may also be a parent, or perhaps an instructor, coach, music teacher, older child, or any adult figure who takes a special interest in us. Through our mentor we are gradually initiated into our gender role. No matter what technical role our mentor plays (teacher, coach, big brother, etc.), our relationship with him increases our confidence with members of our sex outside of our family. His relationship is less nurturing and more instructional. He expects more out of us than our nurturer and challenges us to further develop our masculinity. He provides us with a sort of "rite of passage."

Same-sex *comrades* are vital to a healthy personality. Our comrades mirror us, compete with us, bond with us, and make us feel like "one of the guys." We grow with them, sharing our experiences of school, puberty, dating, social struggles, and so forth. They stabilize us. And our relationship with comrades spurs us on, because we inevitably compare ourselves to them, creating a healthy competition. Through our comrades we learn to feel good about ourselves and comfortable with our own sex.

If we lack any or all of these relationships, we develop what psychologist Elizabeth Moberly calls "same-sex deficits." In her book *Homosexuality: A New Christian Ethic* she stresses the importance of same-sex love between parent and child, and theorizes that the homosexual urge is an attempt to make up for deficiencies in the early father-son, mother-daughter relationship.

Because of those deficiencies, a child may feel that the normal avenues for same-sex love (nurturing, mentoring, comradeship) are not available to him. He thinks, because of parental rejections, that he is not qualified to engage in normal friendships with his peers. This prohibits the very thing he needs the most: love from and closeness to members of the same sex. He wants it so badly, yet he feels that if he tries to get it he will experience further rejection. This leaves him in a quandary: legitimate same-sex intimacy has become the thing he wants the most, yet he avoids the normal activities that provide it because he feels as though any attempts to participate in those activities will fail, leaving him lonely and in pain.

He responds with what Moberly calls "defensive detachment." He detaches himself from his peers and the parent of the same sex because attempting to relate to them causes him pain. Although such relating could be the source of healing for him, he sees it as threatening, avoiding it because he refuses to reexperience the hurt he is sure will come.

He may comfort himself with isolation or by devaluing his father and peers ("They're jerks anyway. Who needs them?"), often rejecting the very masculinity they symbolize. In a way, this protective device works well. By taking no chances, he avoids further rejection. At least he remains emotionally safe.

But his "safety zone" of isolation doesn't kill his ever-deepening need for intimacy. In fact, the more he isolates himself, the stronger that need grows. This is not homosexuality, mind you; rather, it is the legitimate, normal need for bonding that all of us have experienced. In this case, though, the need has grown and remained unsatisfied.

Case in Point: Martin

Martin's father never overtly rejected him. In fact, Martin recalls no specific mistreatment at his father's hands. He worked hard and provided well for his family, but his marriage suffered. His wife longed for more attention than she was getting from her husband (he was reserved, not given to the affectionate expressions she craved), and he resented her requests for more of his time and attention. She responded by withdrawing from her husband and focusing her needs for affection on her son.

Martin was to be a sensitive, intelligent child who provided a listening ear and sympathetic support to his mother, who began confiding in him as she would to a close friend. Confidant, friend, and comforter, Martin learned that his prime function in the home was to "take care of Mom," whose needs were growing as her marriage deteriorated. She began drinking heavily, and Martin began covering up for her and becoming her caretaker. His father, meanwhile, came to resent the bond that mother and son shared, and accordingly withdrew emotionally from both. This only strengthened Martin's conviction that he should stay close to Mom, who seemed to need him so badly. By early adolescence he had virtually no social life; he was too busy at home.

He missed out on all three relationships important to children. He had no male nurturer, no mentor, no comrade. He was by no means effeminate, but he retained a huge need for bonding with his own sex. At times he would fantasize about being in helpless, dangerous situations in which a strong male figure—a superhero of sorts—would come along and rescue him, commending Martin for his bravery and consoling him. This fantasy expressed a desire for male nurturing and mentoring that would continue for years—a desire that was combined with a wish for the type of friendships he saw other boys enjoying. When he entered into his first homosexual relationship, Martin felt that he had finally found the nurturer, mentor, and comrade he had been longing for all his life.

In each of the above cases, certain emotional responses were influenced by the perceptions a child had of himself, his parents, and others of his sex. And these responses inevitably gave way to deep and unsatisfied needs. Emotional responses to early perceptions, whether they take the form of gender identity problems, idealized images, or same-sex deficits, leave a child with specific needs for intimacy with his own sex.

Sexualization of Emotional Needs

Sexual needs are natural to sexual beings. They are the result of the biological drive and the human need for romantic intimacy. There is nothing unhealthy or unusual about them.

Sexualized needs, however, run a different course. These emotional needs are expressed indirectly through sexual activity, acted out through a sort of sexual pantomime. The needs themselves are usually legitimate, but the vehicle used to express them is not. We can see several examples of sexualized emotional needs in everyday life. Plenty of men use sex as a means of reassuring themselves that they are virile, competent, masculine. They delight in sexually conquering women, then bragging about their conquests to other men, causing them to feel manly and complete. Of course, their desire for confidence is a legitimate, understandable one. But sexually exploiting women is an illegitimate means of satisfying that desire. Likewise, many women are promiscuous not because they are sex-starved, but because during sex they are made to feel special and cared for. Again, their needs are perfectly normal, but their method of satisfying those needs is immoral, even dangerous.

This is true of other emotional needs that people express indirectly. Some people, for example, try meeting their need for comfort through food, gorging themselves whenever they are depressed or angry. The use of food has become their emotional outlet, and eating disorders may result. Other people sexualize objects rather than people, finding erotic excitement through fetishes (shoes, leather items, etc.). No one can say exactly why people prefer those methods. All that can be said is that somewhere along the line they found a combination of emotional and sexual fulfillment through unnatural means. What they are seeking—comfort, peace of mind, sexual pleasure—is not wrong in and of itself. It's the way they're seeking it that is unnatural.

Exactly how and under what circumstances do these needs become sexualized? Why are they sexualized in some people but not in others? No one can say for sure. We do know that erotic feelings provide some of our earliest experiences of pleasure. Infants and children explore their bodies, lingering over the body parts that feel especially good. This gives them a sense of warmth and comfort, the "good" spots providing especially pleasurable sensations. I believe that we associate warm, positive feelings with sexual response long before we even know what sex is, because we associate our sexual organs with pleasure and comfort.

It should be no surprise, then, that when a person longs for intimacy with another, that longing may include a desire to share sexual pleasure. For most people, that longing is directed toward members of the opposite sex. Normal development usually includes, as stated earlier, an early phase of bonding with the same sex. By the time this need for same-sex bonding has been satisfied and the child is ready for relations with the opposite sex, he is also entering puberty with its accompanying sexual drives. Perfect timing! Right when we're emotionally prepared for romantic love, our bodies are following suit.

But what happens when we're not emotionally prepared for relationships with the opposite sex? What if, by the time we reach puberty, our need for same-sex love is still unsatisfied and predominant? Our bodies won't wait for our emotions to catch up. Instead, we may develop strong sexual desires which may cross, like wires, with our emotional needs.

In that case, the emotional need for closeness and identification with other people of our sex becomes a sexualized need, with members of our own sex being the object of both our sexual and emotional desires.

And so the emotional responses to early perceptions become sexual responses as well. The need for bonding and identifying with the same sex, accelerated by gender identity problems, becomes a sexual desire. The need to find an ideal male/female figure becomes a need to sexually merge with that figure. And the need for a nurturer, mentor, or comrade becomes a desire for sex with a nurturer, mentor, or comrade.

All of which raises our original question: Why you? No one can say without really knowing both you and your background. But based on what we have seen thus far—some prevalent theories and the experiences of others like you— we can make some educated guesses.

It probably started with your perceptions. You began to see yourself as a child without resources. You know better than I exactly what resources you were lacking: affirmation, attention, a figure to identify with, or maybe a combination of all three. You couldn't articulate it back then; you only knew that something was missing. And that "something" probably centered around a need for a stronger bond with those of your own sex. Maybe you felt different from your peers or alienated from one or both of your parents, most noticeably the one of your own gender. That hurt, no doubt. You wanted closeness; you felt distance. You can't really say, perhaps, who is to bless or who is to blame. Maybe there was obvious rejection; maybe not. But the result is the same either way.

Maybe you responded by withdrawing, creating your own world of safety and fantasy. Or perhaps you simply waited for someone special to love you and take care of you. You may even have become angry, resolving to never again let yourself feel hurt or rejected by another member of your own sex. Each of these responses affected your relationships with other boys/girls and, eventually, with other men and women. You felt different from them, too. They may never have known your feelings of differentness, but you were all too aware of them. They persisted, giving rise to an aching desire to bond, to be close, to feel accepted.

At some point, perhaps very early, maybe later, you realized that this desire was more than emotional. It was accompanied by sexual longings. Most likely, you were aware of those longings before you even knew what homosexuality was. Then one day you heard the word *queer* or *fag,* pondered its meaning, put two and two together, and realized you were one of "them." It became your secret, most likely difficult to keep and even more difficult to bear. You didn't ask for these feelings, but you learned that they were unacceptable to most people. That didn't encourage you to talk them over with anyone, even those closest to you. Your secret became your private burden, one you carried for years. Perhaps even to this day.

So for you, homosexuality, whether expressed through actions or fantasies, represents legitimate emotional needs that have not been satisfied through normal means. You are not mentally ill, reprobate, or retarded. In fact, you may be a highly capable adult who functions well in most areas. But at some point you have found deep satisfaction through homosexual relating.

Remember, homosexuality has served a function for you. Now is the time to do some serious, reflective thinking. What exactly has that function been? What kind of satisfaction have you found through your homosexual fantasies or actions? Only you can answer these questions. When you do, you will know not only what you have been seeking, but also what you still need. Count on it—giving up homosexual contacts will not kill the emotional needs that led to them in the first place. More than ever, you need to meet them legitimately, as fully as possible.

Whatever answers you come up with, you can be sure that what you have been looking for is still available. There are still close relationships to be found, friendships to enjoy, and love and intimacy with the same sex and the opposite sex to be experienced. These are the birthrights of any human, and your hunger for them is God-ordained. They are the vehicles for the security and self-confidence that every child and adult seeks.

Afterthoughts on
Why Me?

It was so easy 12 years ago to write about what fathers should or should not be. I was new to the game, the proud stepfather of a lovably energetic eight-year-old boy, who I'd spent a mere three years actually parenting. Huge mistakes (mostly mine) had not yet been made. His adolescence was years off, so our days were playful and I was his hero, snatching him up after school for bowling, football games, and junk food. No wonder it was so easy for me to look critically at older fathers. I was determined never to become one.

Since then, the boy I loved has become the man who has forgiven me. We jumped into the power struggles and mutual rage every father/son relationship is doomed to, and I careened from rigid strictness to cold fury to indifference, depending on which battle we were fighting. We weathered some tough years, re-bonded, and today I couldn't be prouder of him, or of *us*, when I see the outcome.

But happy ending or not, I know there are things I said and did to him that were damaging and cannot be undone. To some degree, they will affect him and the way he sees life and people. So like all sons, he could write his own book, delivering a rather mixed report card to the old man. I know, too, that what I did not say or do, and should have said or done, cannot be compensated for. In short, I understand more than ever how difficulties between fathers and sons come about. And more than ever, while I stand behind all that is written in this chapter, I also see and stress the need for a forgiving heart.

There is a time for anger, and I will wager you have been reluctant to recognize, much less legitimize, yours. I remember too well the first time I admitted to myself how enraged I was with my own father and how blasphemous and childish I felt. But it was a crucial beginning. Dad is that enormous figure assigned to us who will probably, for better or worse, affect us more profoundly than anyone else in life. So your relationship with him may well play into what you're dealing with now, including your anger. "Be angry, and do not sin" (Ephesians 4:26), Paul advised. It is allowed. If you were wronged, you were hurt; if you were hurt, your anger is justified. So let it come.

Then, in due time, let it go. Because as surely as you need to express and resolve your anger, there will be someone else someday who will need to do the same with his anger toward you. And you, like all of us, are subject to the laws of sowing and reaping. Be sure to sow forgiveness while you can. You will unquestionably be grateful it's there to reap when you need it.

Six

Defining and Experiencing Change

But God is determined to overcome the defacing of His image in us. His plan is not simply to repair most of our brokenness. He wants to make us new creatures. So the story of the human race is not just one of universal disappointment, but one of inextinguishable hope.

—FROM *THE LIFE YOU'VE ALWAYS WANTED* BY JOHN ORTBERG

The idea that homosexuality can be changed is nothing new. The apostle Paul referred to homosexuals when writing to the Corinthian church, then said, "And such *were* some of you" (1 Corinthians 6:11, emphasis added). We cannot believe the Bible without also believing that God redeems His people, forgiving them of sin and freeing them from its dominion over their lives. Homosexuality is no exception.

Although the Bible is authoritative, there are professionals whose opinion has backed up its teaching in this area. Certainly there are mental health practitioners who contend homosexuality is irreversible and simply a normal variation of human sexuality that should be accepted, not changed. But they don't represent the entire profession. So before we discuss the process of change, let's hear from some experts.

> "Despite the rhetoric of homosexual activists, all studies which have attempted conversions from homosexuality to heterosexuality have had significant success"—Dr. Glenn Wood and Dr. John Dietrich.[1]

> "I have recently had occasion to review the result of psychotherapy with homosexuals and been surprised by the findings—a considerable percentage of overt homosexuals became heterosexual"—Reuben Fine.[2]

> "No matter how much remains to be learned in this field, it is evident that people can and do recover from this (homosexuality). Some to a highly satisfactory extent, though not completely, some completely, by all accounts"—Gerard Van Den Aardweg.[3]

> "We have followed some (formerly homosexual) patients for as long as ten years who have remained exclusively heterosexual"—Irving Bieber.[4]

> "I've heard of hundreds of other men who went from a homosexual to a heterosexual adjustment on their own"—Lawrence Hatterer.[5]

> "Each person has to decide where his or her own satisfaction lies; there is no one formula. If the foremost priority in one's life is his religious faith, then his personal happiness might come from conforming to that faith rather than from pursuing his sexual orientation. With human beings, truly anything is possible"—Patricia Hannigan,

president of the Orange County Chapter of the American Psychological Association.[6]

"Recent studies specifically examined religiously-motivated attempts to change sexual orientation. In one study, 248 individuals reported experiencing significantly more heterosexuality than they recalled experiencing at age 18. At a one-year follow-up, 140 of these subjects were re-interviewed and 60.8% of males and 71.1% of females reported behavioral success, defined as abstaining from homosexual contact. Success was associated with strong religious motivation and positive mental health. This provocative new study drew worldwide media attention at the American Psychiatric Association's annual conference on May 9th."[7]

"To the researchers' surprise, good heterosexual functioning was reportedly achieved by 67% of the men who had rarely or never felt any opposite-sex attraction before the change process. Nearly all the subjects said they now feel more masculine."[8]

"'Like most psychiatrists I thought that homosexual behavior could be resisted—but that no one could really change their sexual orientation. I now believe that's untrue—some people can and do change. Contrary to conventional wisdom, some highly motivated individuals, using a variety of change efforts, can make substantial change in multiple indicators of sexual orientation, and achieve good heterosexual functioning.' Spitzer added that change from homosexual to heterosexual is not usually a matter of 'either/or', but exists on a continuum—that is, a diminishing of homosexuality and an expansion of heterosexual potential that is exhibited in widely varying degrees."[9]

(Note: Dr. Spitzer, the researcher quoted here, played an active role in the 1973 American Psychiatric Association's decision to normalize homosexuality, so his remarks here are all the more significant.)

"[Dr. Robert] Epstein said that he had seen some 'interesting data' supporting the ethics and effectiveness of reorientation therapy."[10]*

Sex researchers Masters and Johnson (hardly a pair of standard-bearers for the traditional view!), after offering treatment to homosexual men and women dissatisfied with their orientation, said the "homosexuality cannot be changed" concept was "certainly open to question."[11]

But no one says it better than Stanton Jones, chair of psychology at Wheaton College: "Anyone who says there is no hope (for change) is either ignorant or a liar. Every secular study of change has shown some success rate, and persons who testify to substantial healings by God are legion."[12]

Let me stress again, though, the need for realistic expectations. Change does not occur quickly. In fact, it happens so gradually that you may hardly notice it at first. And, as stated earlier, change occurs to different degrees among different people. Some claim complete conversion of sexual desires from homosexual to heterosexual. Other people experience

---

* The "Epstein" quoted here is Dr. Robert Epstein, the current editor of *Psychology Today* magazine, who recently came under fire from gay rights activists for publicly supporting the rights of homosexuals to seek treatment if they want to change.

reduction, not absence, of homosexual attractions. Still other people allow that, although they are no longer aroused by their own sex, they could backslide or regress to homosexual attractions. Don't compare your process to that of other people, or expect your experience to be exactly like theirs. In this, as in all aspects of life, you are unique.

While deferring to the professional opinions mentioned above, let me add some of my own observations about change.

People definitely can and do change. I think, believe, *know* that to be true. But when they change, it is more often by degrees than by complete transformation.

Alfred Kinsey introduced the concept of a continuum of human sexuality. While I disagree with some of the other conclusions he drew in his 1948 study of male sexuality, I do think this concept of continuum is valuable and true.[13] People experience sexual attractions to a certain degree of frequency and intensity on a scale as listed here:

0   Exclusively heterosexual, no homosexual attractions

1   Predominantly heterosexual, incidental homosexual attractions

2   Predominantly heterosexual, more than incidental homosexual attractions

3   Equally heterosexual and homosexual attractions

4   Predominantly homosexual, more than incidental heterosexual attractions

5   Predominantly homosexual, incidental heterosexual attractions

6   Exclusively homosexual attractions[14]

"Males do not represent two populations, heterosexual and homosexual," Kinsey said. "Not all things are black nor all things white."[15] That is exactly why I dislike the term *homosexual* when used as a noun. People are not really homosexual or heterosexual, as I see it, but they are people who have, to some degree, homosexual or heterosexual attractions, or a combination of each. In this sense, homosexuality is best used as an adjective to describe feelings, not people.

If homosexual attractions exist to degrees, I believe they also change by degrees. So a person who rates a Kinsey 6 is not likely to jump right into point 1 or 0 (though I can't deny the possibility), but will instead change more gradually, point to point. How far will he go? How long will it take? No one can say. But I'm convinced this change will follow the principle of a continuum; that is, he will experience homosexual desires to a lesser degree. They will become less predominant, giving way to a higher degree of and potential for heterosexual desires. No one can predict the limit or the extent to which this change takes place, but it is by degrees.

Process

How then does change happen? I see it occur in a five-point process:

1. Homosexual behavior ceases.

2. Needs that have been satisfied through homosexuality are heightened and identified.

3. Nonsexual intimacy begins to satisfy identified needs.

4. Self-perception changes.

5. Sexualized emotional response to early perceptions changes.

Let's look at this process in more detail.

First, *homosexual behavior ceases.* This is necessary for two reasons: one, homosexual acts are sinful, and sin stunts emotional growth because it pollutes the entire personality. It increases guilt, weakens faith, and leads to depression (and often to despair). No one can grow successfully when willfully committing sexual sins. Two: if homosexuality has served as a function to fulfill certain needs, it logically follows that, as long as a person continues to commit homosexual acts, then the needs they fulfill will be repressed. Viewed this way, homosexual behavior is like holding a basketball underwater. As long as the ball is held down, it won't come to the surface. When it's released, it will show itself. So it is with the emotional needs that lie behind homosexuality. They cannot be clearly identified as long as homosexual behavior holds them "underwater," beneath consciousness. And as long as they remain unidentified, they cannot be recognized and legitimately fulfilled.

Second, *needs that have been satisfied through homosexuality are heightened and identified.* When the basketball is released, it bobs to the surface and is easier than ever to identify. And when homosexual behavior is removed, the needs behind it become more acute than ever. That's why many people have such a difficult time abstaining from sexual "acting out." It's not just sexual temptation that draws them back, but the desire to satisfy these needs in the old, tried-and-true way. Some would say that few people really change because homosexuality is so deeply ingrained. I'm more inclined to think that many people give up at this point because they refuse to tolerate the frustration of feeling unsatisfied emotional needs. Like the children of Israel wandering in the desert, they long for their familiar past and the satisfaction it gave them.

"I never knew how hooked I was on sexual acting out until I gave it up," a counselee once told me. "Since then I've felt more lonely and depressed than ever. It doesn't seem fair that I've given up something that's wrong but still feel all these conflicts. It just makes me want to go back. I don't really want to do it with a man again, I just want to stop the pain."

Using the model of homosexual development I proposed in the last chapter, suppose a man's homosexual behavior satisfied his need for a nurturing male to take care of him. He turns away from this behavior, only to find that he needs such a nurturer more than ever. But the only way he has gotten that nurturing in the past is through homosexuality. He hasn't yet learned nonsexual ways of getting what he needs, so he goes through a season of waiting while the need continues to throb away. It almost seems cruel—"unfair," as my counselee said.

But that is exactly how legitimate needs are eventually satisfied! First they make themselves known. Only then can a person plan legitimate, nonsexual ways to satisfy them. Another counselee put it well:

> I thought I wanted sex. I still do, I guess, but more than that I want to feel special to somebody. I want to feel that a man really cares whether I live or die. I want to know that I have at least one person who's close to me and really accepts me as I am. And I want that person to be somebody who's "together," not just some loser who'll latch on to anybody. I want to feel honest-to-God accepted by a man I can look up to. In fact, I want to be like that man.

Then *nonsexual intimacy begins to satisfy identified needs.* The frustration of unmet needs motivates a man to look for alternative, nonsexual ways to meet them. This often means conquering his long-held fear of his own sex. When he confronts that fear by allowing himself nonsexual closeness with other men, he finds healing in that closeness. He begins to feel significance, the security or affection he sought in homosexual relationships, and he learns that sex is not the only way to obtain those feelings. This is when real healing begins—when a person receives through normal relationships the benefits he used to get through abnormal ones.

Fourth, *self-perception changes.* The early perceptions I mentioned came about through early relationships. In a faulty parent-child relationship, for example, the child might have perceived his parent to have a certain attitude toward him ("Dad doesn't like me." "Dad thinks I'm unimportant."), which he then internalized or came to believe about himself ("I'm not likable." "I'm unimportant."). These are perceptions based on what the child assumed his parent thought about him. When, as an adult, he allows other important figures to relate to him, he begins to internalize *their* thoughts toward him. ("This person values me as an equal, not as a sexual partner or a subordinate. If he thinks I'm valuable, maybe I really am valuable!") That is the power of healthy friendship. It revolutionizes the way we see ourselves, because it provides proof that someone else thinks we are worth spending time with and being close to. And when that closeness is nonsexual, it challenges our belief that sex is the primary way to feel same-sex closeness.

Then, *sexualized emotional response to early perceptions changes.* When a perception changes, the response has to follow suit. So if a person has perceived people of his own sex as being distant and inaccessible, he will respond with an intense longing for same-sex closeness. Likewise, if through normal friendships instead of homosexual relations he learns that his peers will love and accept him, his need for same-sex closeness will diminish. It will partially remain, of course, because to some degree we will always need to bond with members of our own sex. But the need for that bonding will be less intense.

Intimacy with our peers is like water; we always need it. But if we have gone without it for a long period, our need for it turns into a craving that will drive us to do almost anything to get it. We may even drink seawater or gutter water if our thirst is intense enough and we don't think there is any other way to satisfy it. When a strong emotional need has been sexualized, its satisfaction can be sought in a number of illegitimate ways, including homosexuality. But when that need is being met legitimately, homosexual behavior holds less appeal. That, too, is a sign of real change.

At this point there may still be homosexual attractions, even when the problems that originally created them are being resolved. Often these attractions have become learned responses to a certain stimulus, a kind of knee-jerk reaction. But when knee-jerk reactions are not reinforced through repetition, they diminish. If they have been learned, they can also be unlearned.

This process of change is dependent on relationships that are close and nonsexual. And so the process of the development of homosexuality and change comes full circle. The problem *started* in a relationship and is *resolved* through relationships. I can't overemphasize this point: All of the prayer, insight, and effort you can muster will not change your sexual desires one bit if you don't establish the kind of relationships you need. Homosexuality is an attempt to satisfy yourself through an unhealthy relationship. Now is the time to learn how to satisfy yourself through healthy ones.

Afterthoughts on
Defining and Experiencing Change

I wasn't thinking about change when I prayed in the dark and repented that January evening of 1984. I was thinking about the forgiveness I needed and the obedience I was committing to. If I did ask God to change anything that night, it was my will and my weakness. I had never heard of or considered a change in sexual orientation.

And I'm glad I hadn't, because the "change" issue, while important, can be a distraction.

It's distracting, especially if priorities are imbalanced. Just as the "how" is more important then the "why," so the issue of obedience is more important than the degree to which attractions can change. When God calls a man to repent of a sin, He is fully aware of whatever psychological or genetic influences may have created an inclination toward that sin. Likewise, He considers how deeply ingrained the sin may be, and how long—perhaps a lifetime—the man may be drawn toward it. None of this amends or weakens God's commandment to repent.

A more biblical view of sin recognizes the difference between the *presence* of sin and the *power* of sin. Its presence is guaranteed, no matter how godly the man. John, in fact, said a man who thinks he has no sin is kidding himself (1 John 1:8). And Paul, even though established as an apostle and revered leader, recognized the need to be mindful of his ongoing sinful tendencies and the havoc they could wreak on him and his ministry if he left them unchecked (1 Corinthians 9:27). That is the sad reality of the presence of sin.

131

Yet Paul balances this out with a hopeful perspective: "Sin shall not have dominion over you" (Romans 6:14). So a Christian goes through life recognizing some degree of temptation, probably on a daily basis. But he also notices the temptations are less severe, less frequent, and certainly not overpowering. That is the happy reality of sin's diminished power.

For this reason, I have never liked the term *ex-gay*. It's accurate to an extent, if *gay* means "openly homosexual and comfortable with it." By that definition, many people have rejected homosexual behavior and a "gay-positive" identity. But if *gay* is used to simply mean "homosexual," then the term *ex-gay* implies that a person who *was* homosexual now has *no* homosexual attractions. And that is, at the very least, misleading.

So while I have never been exclusively attracted to men, and was, in fact, sexually attracted to girls and women from early in life, I could still be drawn toward same-sex encounters. If I placed myself in an environment (a gay bar, for example, or gay-oriented gym) where men were being overtly sexual with each other, that would reawaken old desires which I would obviously prefer to let sleep. A man who is truly and exclusively heterosexual could not say the same. So for that reason, I have to regard myself as subject to temptation, and live, like Paul, with a reasonable caution.

Yet to imply there has been no change in my behavior and attractions since 1984 is laughable. I stopped all sexual relations with men in January of that year, along with pornography and the use of male and female prostitutes. My wife and I dated three years (which is two-and-a-half years longer than I lasted with any man) before marriage, and have enjoyed a monogamous relationship, a fulfilling sex life, and a partnership I would match against anyone's. In that sense, I'm much like a 5'10" guy who weighed 500 pounds, then lost 250 of them. He is still overweight, but could you honestly say that even though he retains some fat, he hasn't changed?

You can and will change. In this life, the change will be real, if incomplete. But, thank God, your eternal reward is determined by your obedience when tempted, not by the presence—or lack—of homosexual temptations. "Blessed is the man who endures temptation," James said, "for…he will receive a crown of life which the Lord has promised to those who love Him" (James 1:12).

So for every change you notice in your attractions or behavior, thank God for the blessing you are experiencing in this life. And for every temptation you recognize and resist, thank God for the reward you will experience in the next.

Seven

Maintaining
Sexual Integrity

*Between stimulus and response, there is a space. In that
space is our power to choose our response. In our response lies
our growth and our freedom.*

—FROM *FIRST THINGS FIRST* BY STEPHEN COVEY

Here's an unflattering thought to consider: Everything
is in a constant state of decay. Without maintenance, things
deteriorate. So do people. So will you. If you can accept that
fact, you will avoid the apathy that can keep a man from
maintaining his sexual integrity.

Not convinced? Look at your yard. It isn't naturally
inclined toward beauty. It has beauty's potential, but to bring
that potential out you have to keep it from doing what it's
naturally inclined to do: grow weeds, dry out, die. How about
your body? It's a great machine, but it's not naturally inclined
to stay in shape. If you want to avoid obesity, scruffiness, or
body odor, you have to work on it, exercising and grooming
your body daily. The same can be said of almost anything:

pets, finances, houses. Without constant attention and maintenance, things naturally decay.

The gains you make toward sexual wholeness are also subject to decay. Every new level of maturity you achieve will be challenged, because you live in a fallen world, one that is hardly sympathetic to your commitment to purity. That's one reason sexual temptations linger after repentance, no matter how earnest the repentance has been.

I'm not suggesting you go through life paranoid, or that you keep looking over your shoulder to catch an oncoming temptation before it catches you. I'm only warning you to guard your integrity.

Sexual integrity is a state of consistency in which your sexual expressions are consistent with God's standards. It is again a question of stewardship. You have repented of sexual *sin;* you have not repented of being a sexual *man,* with sexual passions and drive. Which means you are still responsible to keep them under control and reserved for their proper use.

After repentance there is usually a period of real joy. A clear conscience, a sense of freedom, and newfound optimism make a powerful combination. You feel zealous, eager to make a new start. And when, through enlightenment, you learn about yourself and finally get answers to some long-held questions, that is doubly exciting. It frees you up, giving you that "Aha!" kind of feeling ("Now I finally understand!"). This phase is so energizing that many people mistake it for a complete deliverance from sexual temptations. "Now that I've given up my sin, and understand why I got involved with it in the first place, I know I could never go back," they say. On the one hand, that's a great attitude. It's a legitimate high. But it's also, sad to say, a temporary stage. Sooner or later temptations will come, and the rather mundane task of day-to-day maintenance replaces the under-standable but unrealistic exhilaration.

This is nothing new. Jesus Himself said that many people receive the Word with great joy for a season, but if they have no root in themselves, they fall away when tribulation comes. Not *if* it comes; *when* it comes! So the best defense against falling away is maintenance.

Sexual integrity is an act of the will, expressed through day-to-day decisions. It's really that simple. Whether you succeed or fail in this area will be determined by your will-ingness to make and stick to daily decisions to keep your sex life consistent with your standards. (Yes, you do have a sex life, whether you're sexually active or not. As long as you have sexual desires, you have a sex life.)

It's also a matter of strategy. Integrity is maintained when you have a predetermined plan for dealing with the sexual temptations to which you are most prone. It's like garden-ing. To keep a yard up, you need to pay attention to main-tenance, keeping the yard free of weeds, leaves, or any elements which prohibit healthy growth.

So even after making a new start, certain elements—weeds, of sorts—should be watched for and guarded against. Anyone who makes a major change has weeds to deal with: traces of old behavior, times of discouragement, and patterns to break. You may also find you have your own special "weeds." Common among these are addictive sexual behavior, inner and homoerotic relationships.

Compulsive/Addictive Behavior

Addictive sexual behavior is no joke. It includes lust and poor self-control, of course, but it is much more than that. It is a repetitive, constant form of sexual activity that a person feels *compelled*—not just tempted—to indulge in. Usually this behavior is acted out in secretive, anonymous sexual encounters in parks, public bathrooms, or adult bookstores. Seldom does it include one lover; most often it means brief trysts with several partners, most of whom will never be seen again. Or it may be a solitary addiction to pornography. Regardless, it's a bondage of the worst kind because there is so much shame and remorse attached to it, making it terribly secretive and usually dangerous. It leads to arrest, broken marriages, and untold humiliation. If you have been hooked into it, you know that repentance alone won't stop it, although repentance is necessary. You have tried to stop before, I'm sure. Now that you're addressing the whole spectrum of your homosexual experiences, you are no doubt as serious as ever about breaking free. For that alone you deserve encouragement and wholehearted support. But you may feel reluctant to look for it because secrecy, as well as compulsivity, is part of your problem.

Sexually addictive behavior is highly secretive. When you are caught up in it, you're not prone to discuss it with anyone, so friends and family members seldom know what you're going through. It's a double life of sorts, involving a public image of normality versus a long-held secret. Usually the man discovers his "drug" relatively early in life, becomes dependent on it, and incorporates it into his behavioral makeup. If that's true of you, you are carrying a heavy load. You haven't felt good about your behavior or yourself, but have had no idea how to change. What you *do* know how to do is hide, and at that I will bet you're a pro. The years of secret-keeping, excuses for prolonged absences from job and family while you're having sex, and lying to cover your tracks have taught you to conceal your actions and feelings. Besides the destructiveness of your actions, you suffered from an unwillingness to let anyone in.

Even if you have stopped—repented—you should realize by now the cycles addictions can go through. I won't presume to say your repentance does no good, or that you are inevitably going to fall into your old patterns again. I will only say that addicts of any kind should get help, because the problems that led to their addiction, just like the problems that lead to homosexuality, need to be settled before the condition will lose its power. "Just Say No" is a great start. But more needs to be done.

Let someone in immediately. You have developed a private world centered around your addiction, and the privacy is what's keeping it intact. Disrupt the privacy of your world, and you weaken both it and the addiction it protects. You will be less inclined to repeat the behavior you have given up if you know someone else is involved in your struggle with you.

A trained Christian professional with experience treating addictions will be valuable to you. As always, you should get a referral from your pastor or a trusted friend, if possible. But do find qualified help. With it, you can understand the roots of your addiction and build up the defenses against destructive actions—defenses that have been torn down over the years.

You also should get into a support group—a Christ-centered one—that is geared toward this problem. This provides you with a legitimate emotional outlet for the conflicting feelings you will experience while you withdraw from your addiction. And finally, get some accountability. To be accountable to someone means to let him in on your struggle and keep him up on your progress. It's a giving over of your right to privacy to at least one person who has your permission to question you about your day-to-day activities and encourage you when you struggle. You may balk at this, thinking it's too oppressive, too childish. But don't kid yourself—you can't deal with sexually compulsive behavior by yourself. If you could, you would have done so long ago.

Inward Pollution

Inward pollution is a much more common struggle—so common, in fact, I would say it's almost universal. Your inner man is going to be attacked by two formidable challengers: erotic images and memories of past sexual encounters. Both of these are powerful opponents; both can be faced and conquered.

Erotic images pose a challenge. I dare you to try to escape them. There was a time you could do so pretty easily just by avoiding pornographic magazines, but those days are long gone. Take a drive and you'll see some model flashing his wares on a billboard. Thumb through a magazine—a *regular* magazine, mind you—and you'll get hit with clothing ads that show more flesh than clothes. Watch television and you won't get away from sexual themes no matter what channel you turn to. Try as you may, you can't get away from erotic images without going into hibernation. You are a prisoner in a cult of physical beauty, and the gods and goddesses of the Perfect Physique demand your attention wherever you are.

You probably respond to erotic images according to a cycle: visual contact, stimulation, sexual arousal. You notice or "flash on" a picture that gets your attention, whether or not you want it to. There's a quick charge of stimulation, a recognition of the kind of image that excites you. You feel pulled into the image, prone to linger over it and consume it. Sexual arousal follows, with a drive to unite with the image in a mental sexual encounter.

You can abort this cycle through simple decision-making. Go back to rule one: Integrity is a process of daily decisions to remain consistent with your beliefs. Nine times out of ten, you didn't decide to flash onto the magazine picture, billboard, or shirtless guy walking down the street. It was there, so you saw it. At the moment of recognition, though ("Wow, he's just my type!"), you can decide to move on. The earlier you decide, the easier it is not to be obsessed with the image. Your responsibility is not to keep good-looking bodies out of your field of vision (an impossibility) or to force yourself not to be attracted by them. Rather, you're responsible to keep moving, not letting yourself dwell on what you are seeing.

Once you've torn your eyes away, there is still the mental image of what you've seen and the sexual response that has already kicked into gear. Some call it "going into heat"—I guess that phrase will do. When you're in heat, you burn. It can't be helped. Your responsibility is to contain the burning and yourself by not letting it dictate to your body what it's going to do. ("My body belongs to me. I don't belong to it.") You grow considerably by doing this, because you exercise the emotional muscles of self-restraint and mental discipline. The payoffs are incredible.

Coming out on the winning side of a sexual temptation, though, is only part of what you need to deal with when you're aroused by sexual images. The other dragon you have to fight is your own frustration. Men resisting same-sex temptations can get so focused on being "cured" of homosexuality that they judge their entire well-being by the frequency and intensity of their same-sex attractions. "Not again!" they scream. "I can't believe that person turned me on. I'm so sick of this. How could those feelings still be there? I'm such a failure!"

The truth is, you're only a failure if you haven't done what you were able to do. Yours is not the responsibility of changing your feelings. You can't anyway; you should know that by now. Instead, you have to concentrate on taking steps that will promote growth—correcting habits, setting relationships right, disciplining yourself to maintain your integrity—and let the growth come in its time. If it's slow in coming, that's not your fault. And beating yourself up over it will only frustrate the process. So instead of wringing your hands over your responses to erotic images, I suggest you learn from them. Yes, learn from them, because they could very well be a representation of the qualities you feel you lack—qualities which you should pursue and strengthen.

You may be surprised to hear that the images arousing you are only complementing an erotic image that was formed in your mind long ago. This image is a combination of people you have actually seen who made an impact on you, figures you have fantasized about, and bodily representations of concepts of masculinity that appeal to you. That's why certain "types" of people attract us. They remind us of our inner image—the bodily representation of characteristics that appeal to us.

Images are more like mirages than mirrors. Mirrors reflect what we are, while mirages represent what we need. (A thirsty man in the desert needs water, sees a mirage...you know the story.) Often we use these images in private fantasy to give us comfort, heightened pleasure, or a sense of completion.

"No," you say. "I just use them to feel turned on." Okay, I'll buy that. But that "turned-on" state is, I believe, another example of sexualized need. The images have a sexual quality, but they embody concepts we want to touch or merge with emotionally. Our needs at some point have become sexualized, and so the desire to emotionally bond with a certain "type" becomes a sexualized desire.[1]

Case in Point: Larry

Larry's story provides a good example. The concepts of male strength held tremendous appeal to young Larry. He recalls his father as a kind but remarkably passive man, the son of a man who was similarly meek, quiet, and agreeable. His mother stood in sharp contrast. The world was her territory, and she knew it. She took charge of every situation, controlled all conversations, made all decisions, and unmercifully criticized those around her. Interestingly enough, Larry didn't so much resent her for this as he resented his father for allowing it. He felt that a man should be stronger than that and longed for such a man to look up to and gain his own strength from.

That man came to him, not in person but through a western film Larry saw when he was seven. In it, the hero showed himself to be everything Larry felt that he, his father, and all men should be: strong, conquering, able to stand his ground against anyone. Larry was enthralled, idolizing this obviously exaggerated form of masculinity, as boys often do.

Midway through the movie, the hero whipped his shirt off, displaying the classic Hollywood he-man physique. Larry recalls no sexual feelings for the man at the time, but remembers deciding there was a direct link between a well-developed male body and all the concepts of masculinity he wanted to get close to and eventually have himself. The image stayed, became sexualized later, and jelled into homosexual desires. In this case, the image was a mirage, an unreal representation of what Larry felt he needed.

Dr. Moberly calls this "cannibalism"—a concept she describes as a means of "consuming" a person (or image) sexually and thereby having the qualities he has, qualities which the "consumer" thinks he lacks (Moberly, 1983). Erotic homosexual images can serve this purpose. They provide a concrete, bodily representation of qualities a man thinks he lacks and unknowingly tries to obtain through a sexual merge. (Many of my clients, for example, have been especially attracted to a big brother or father image. Not coincidentally, their relationships with their fathers were unsatisfactory.)

I'm not advising you to stop and analyze pictures of good-looking men just to see what emotional needs you're trying to fulfill by sexually merging with them! But it is helpful to understand the reason these images have such appeal. When you do, you can begin working to adopt those qualities for yourself.

Erotic imagery needn't be blatantly sexual. The attraction to another person you see in day-to-day life can also be considered a struggle with imagery. Sometimes men are especially discouraged by the attractions they feel for people they see. The "looking syndrome" has them baffled. "How can I ever stop looking at attractive people when they're all around me?" they moan.

First, let's make a distinction between looking and lusting. It's no sin to notice the fact that a person is good-looking. Everyone does that, whether they admit it or not. I find that men are especially hung up about this, and needlessly so. Most women feel quite free to openly admire another attractive woman. My wife, for example, will always spot a pretty woman in the room. She doesn't hesitate to comment on the other woman's hair, makeup, or figure. And she is certainly not lusting! Men, as well, do notice other attractive men. Noticing a man's good looks is no more perverted than noticing his new car or fancy suit. All it means is that your eyeballs are working.

You may, of course, be doing more "serious" looking than the man who has never had homosexual attractions. So the second question to ask yourself is this: Are you lusting after another man or envying him? Are you comparing yourself to him to see how you match up? Believe it or not, that's what a lot of "cruising" is all about—comparisons.

If that's the case, what exactly is it that you admire about him? His mannerisms? Physique? Features? Does he have something that you want for yourself? That's not necessarily bad, if it spurs you on to improve yourself in the areas that you can realistically improve. (Some people would argue that as Christians we shouldn't be overly concerned about our appearance. I'm not so sure. If improving your physique or grooming will feed your masculine confidence, I say, "Go for it!")

Finally, if after ruling out the other possibilities, you have to admit that you are simply lusting, don't wallow in it. Confess it to God and yourself, then move on. Don't beat yourself up over a simple learned response to attractive people. I've come to believe that a man's obsession with his attractions ("They're still there, darn it!") creates a bigger problem for him than the attractions themselves. What I've stated earlier bears repeating: It is no sin to be homosexually attracted. It only becomes a sin when you act upon or deliberately feed that attraction. It is up to God, not you, to diffuse those attractions, so don't take responsibility for what you cannot control. You have enough responsibilities to contend with as it is.

Memories

Your past includes a whole repertoire of sexual fantasies and experiences. Though you have put those experiences behind you, you have not, nor will you ever, banish them from your memory. They stay in your mind like an old movie, ready to be replayed and reviewed time and again. In a sense they're like a handy piece of pornography you can always pull out and browse through. They're not just passive, either. They won't wait for you to refer to them. They will intrude into your thoughts like unwelcome burglars, robbing you of a sound mind and clear thinking.

The past uses your memory to keep itself alive, attacking your integrity by reminding you how "good" it all was, or by condemning you with the memory of how bad it all was. Either way, old mental tapes are a constant nuisance to be dealt with.

Also, your past reminds you of a concrete way of dealing with loneliness, boredom, anger, or any number of negative feelings. It invites you to return to the old faithful method for getting temporary gratification, and you're especially susceptible to that invitation when you're not at your best. (Another good reason to be watchful.)

Assuming you have recently turned from homosexual activity, you're in a sort of Twilight Zone. That's neither bad nor good; it just is. You've given up a sexual function which made you feel complete, satisfied, beloved. It's a good thing you gave it up, of course. The problem is, you may not have found alternative methods—acceptable ones, that is—that will give you the same sense of satisfaction. So when you're hit with pressures, mood swings, or anxieties, your past urges you to go back to the coping mechanisms (homosexual activity) which have proven to be somewhat effective. Sinful, yes, but still temporarily effective. The allure of those effective methods also gnaws away at your integrity.

The Good Old Days always look better in retrospect, especially when you're having Bad New Days. But isn't the fact that you're having struggles proof that you're stretching? Stretching isn't always fun. You stretch when you force yourself to try new behaviors, or when you deny yourself what you used to indulge in. When you stretch yourself, you exercise patience. And when stretching, you force yourself to go a little further than you've gone before. You get tired, so naturally your thoughts turn toward the days when you weren't stretching—days when you indulged. And, of course, your thoughts turn toward the indulgence itself.

Whether the past holds the memory of one particular lover or of pleasurable times in general, it takes on an enchanting quality. It makes you feel your current life is empty, unsatisfying, and therefore fruitless.

Like the "heat" of arousal, these periods of looking back and longing for something different are usually cyclic. David had a similar experience when he envied the seemingly terrific lives of wicked people. "I was envious of the boastful, when I saw the prosperity of the wicked," he wrote in Psalm 73. Describing their strength and success, even when committing evil deeds, he concluded, "I have cleansed my heart in vain, and washed my hands in innocence." (Translation: "What good is godly living when the ungodly have it so much better? And what's the use in giving up ungodliness when it seems to provide more happiness than righteousness? Righteousness doesn't keep me warm at night!")

Then David looked ahead a little and considered not the good life the wicked enjoyed, but the end result of it. And it hit him like cold water: "Oh, how they are brought to desolation, as in a moment!" The value of right living, he concluded, is not its present satisfaction, though there is that as well, but its long-range benefits.

The value in leaving an ungodly though pleasurable past is that it has no future. Your memories look good only because you're not seeing them panoramically. Take them to their logical conclusion, considering not only what you did and enjoyed, but where it was leading you, and you get a more accurate picture of your past. That's how you shake off the power of "good" memories—you view them with an eternal perspective.

Masturbation

Any discussion of male sexual purity has to include masturbation. It's one of the earliest forms of sexual expression we experience and the commonest form of sexual activity among humans. Yet it is seldom discussed, widely misunderstood, and is a universally embarrassing topic. So let's hit the question head-on: Is it all right for you to masturbate?

Let's recognize, first, that there are no specific references to masturbation in the Bible. Some people mistakenly quote Genesis chapter 38, the story of Onan who "spilled his seed onto the ground," as a reference to masturbation. But a closer look at the text shows that Onan was in the middle of sexual intercourse, then withdrew just before ejaculating, thereby "spilling his seed on the ground" to avoid impregnating his wife. He wasn't masturbating; he was practicing a crude form of birth control.

Since there are no clear biblical prohibitions against masturbation, we can't say that the Bible specifically condemns it, but I would offer at least three cases in which I would consider masturbation to be sinful.

First, since 1 Corinthians 7:4 teaches, in reference to sex in marriage, that a husband's body "belongs" to his wife, I believe it's wrong for a married man to masturbate. In doing so, he is taking what belongs to his wife and using it only for himself, which seems a violation of Paul's guideline in this verse.

Second, since Jesus condemned internal lust (fantasies, etc.) in Matthew 5:28, then if it is impossible for a man to masturbate without fantasizing, for him masturbation is a sin.

Finally, since Paul said that anything a man does without faith—that is, anything a man does that he feels badly about even if it's not forbidden in Scripture—is for him a sin (Romans 14:23). So even if a man is single and has the ability to masturbate without fantasizing, if he feels it's wrong for him to masturbate, then for him it *is* wrong.

Which raises the question of how *you* feel about masturbation. Even though God doesn't necessarily prohibit it, if your own conscience is violated by it, it has become a sin for you. Paul said, "Whatever is not from faith is sin." In other words, if you believe a behavior is wrong, you have to abstain from it whether it's biblically prohibited or not. If you feel masturbation is wrong for you, the argument stops there. It's not an option.

Within these guidelines, you can make your own decision about masturbation. While it's not necessarily condemned in all cases, it's certainly not commended, either. Marital status, conscience, sexual fantasy, and common sense should all play into your decision on this controversial and highly personal question.

A Sound Defense

The best offense is a good defense. So battling inward pollution is best done by keeping the inner man clean, or spiritually minded. Paul illustrated the struggle between the flesh and the Spirit in Galatians 5:17 by calling it a war between the two. They do battle with each other incessantly, so that you never seem to keep your thoughts as clean as you would like to. The trick is not to concentrate only on the negative (lustful thoughts) but to emphasize the positive. Paul's solution? "Walk in the Spirit, and you shall not fulfill the lust of the flesh" (Galatians 5:16). Practically speaking, that means a life of consistent inward prayer.

To be in constant prayer doesn't mean living like a monk. Instead, it means a consistent awareness of God's presence, plus nonstop acknowledgment of His nearness to you and residence within you. It means instant confession of sin when it occurs and a commitment to keep your thoughts centered on Him. Keeping the mind centered on God—His nearness, His goodness, and His unfailing love for you—is the best defense against mental impurity that I know of.

Pastor Chuck Smith of Calvary Chapel in Costa Mesa, California, used to describe the futility of merely trying to drive dark forces out of your life. He compared it to being in a darkened room. "When you're in the dark," he would say, "it won't do any good to walk around with a baseball bat trying to drive the darkness out. Instead, try turning on the light."

Walk in the Spirit—with the lights turned on—and inward pollution will not control you.

Homoerotic Attractions

Homoerotic relationships are distinct from homosexual ones in that they don't necessarily include sex, but they do include strong, mutual erotic attractions.

These situations—homoerotic entanglements—can arise when two men are part of a support group or specialized ministry dealing with homosexuality. They are drawn to each other—perhaps innocently at first, perhaps not. At times they are completely unaware of their attraction, only to find it cropping up in spite of their best intentions. At other times they've just been kidding themselves. They were sexually turned on to each other from the word "go" and pretended they were really just interested in brotherly love and support. In either case, the two are enmeshed in a sensitive, dangerous communion of desire and dependency. What began as a seemingly godly friendship has turned into a snare. Should they consummate their lust, the repercussions are extreme.

It can happen to anybody. It does happen, in fact, among people of all orientations. Pastors and therapists fall into sexual relations with their counselees, church members develop attractions for each other, sympathetic husbands become too involved with the problems of another man's wife. An affair is seldom the original plan. It gradually evolves when both parties refuse to recognize the erotic longings growing between them.

So don't consider yourself immune to this. More to the point, adopt this commandment: Thou Shalt Not Kid Thyself. If and when you recognize strong attractions for another man, call them what they are. They're not a special "Jonathan and David" kind of love. They're not the beginning of a special friendship. They are, in fact, erotic attractions that can lead you and the other party to ruin. You know they're present when you become mildly obsessed with another person, having to spend extra time with him at every support group meeting or church service, needing to know he likes you and wants your company. When you require a long hug from him every time you say "hello," watch it. And if you're thinking about him constantly during the week, don't pretend there's no problem.

Instead, use common sense. You needn't flog yourself over this situation; it's understandable, though undesirable. But don't ignore it, either. Although there's not a hard-and-fast rule for handling this, let me offer some suggestions.

By the way, don't assume you should admit your attraction to another man. Maybe you feel you should be honest, but consider this: By disclosing your feelings to him, you may well set up a stumbling block for him as well as yourself. If he is likewise attracted to you, you might be inflaming the very spark he wants to put out. I would advise, instead, that you disclose this to your group leader, pastor, or whomever you're accountable to. Ask for that person's honest counsel and let him be a part of your struggle through this.

Avoid having an exclusive relationship with a man who is dealing with homosexuality. That only solidifies the problem. When you're together, include other people as well. Keep up your other friendships and you will be less likely to invest all your affections in him.

And speaking of common sense, don't be foolish enough to spend time alone with a person you're attracted to, especially if you sense the attraction is mutual. That's not only wrong, but just plain stupid. Draw clear boundaries and stick to them. That's a part of the day-to-day decision-making that goes with sexual integrity—the decision not to do what you feel the most compelled to do at any given time.

Don't assume that a homoerotic relationship will last forever. If the two of you are sincere, and act on your sincerity, the attractions will diminish. Most likely they are idealizations, unrealistic and temporary, which will fade in time. Explore your response to this person with your counselor or pastor, and you might find it springs from an emptiness of your own which you're trying to fill with the erotic love of another. And so this relationship may actually become beneficial to you if it indicates an area of yours that requires attention.

In Case of Emergency

Hopefully you will maintain your integrity in the face of temptation. But there is the possibility that, in a time of stress or weakness, you will fail. In that case, what happens when the runner stumbles? If he's smart, he'll get back on the track ASAP.

You may stumble. It's a pretty serious thing to do, and there's no justification for it. You don't have to fall. Unless you were forcibly abducted, you certainly had the ability to say no to a sexual invitation. But should it happen, remember that your main goal, like the runner's, is to get back into the race.

Avoid the equally futile extremes of ignoring a sexual fall or wallowing in guilt over it. To ignore a sin is to pretend it's no sin at all, and you only deceive yourself with that approach. Until it's acknowledged, it can't be dealt with, and until it's dealt with, it can't be left behind. Wallowing in guilt over a fall is just as useless. Years of self-reproach won't undo a scrap of the damage, so put the whip away. Full atonement for sin was made at the cross. Do you really think you can do better than that?

Instead, confess the sin immediately. That's how you're cleansed and forgiven. Confession to God is an acknowledgment that you have offended Him, as well as an admission of your inability to undo the wrong. The moment confession is made, fellowship with God is restored. Jesus wasn't kidding, after all, when He said that anyone who comes to Him will in no wise be cast out.

Integrity—the decision to remain consistent with your standards (and God's)—is made up of hundreds of small, moment-to-moment decisions. And each decision, when followed through, strengthens you to make another one. Success breeds success. And what is it you're trying to succeed at?

You're trying and learning to be governed by your convictions instead of by your feelings. *That is the ultimate goal of maintaining sexual integrity.* Man was created to enjoy his passions, never to be ruled by them. So each decision to act out of conviction feeds your sense of integrity and, by extension, your freedom to follow your convictions.

Self-respect, an important quality for anyone, is built up by maintaining your integrity. Ironically, the maintenance of sexual integrity, though it appears to be self-denial, is in fact self-fulfilling—permanently, deeply so.

God's commandments were given not to restrict our lives, but to make them free in the truest sense of all.

Afterthoughts on
Maintaining Sexual Integrity

If I were writing this chapter today, I would put more emphasis on the nature and the power of accountability. If maintaining integrity is our goal, we will reach it only by admitting how little integrity we have when left on our own, how much more we need, and how dependent we are on each other to provide additional integrity.

When speaking at a Promise Keepers' conference some years ago, I was required (as all the speakers were) to wear a shirt with the words "Men of Integrity" emblazoned across the front. I pulled it on, checked the mirror, and felt a little funny. "Men of Integrity" looked good, but on me it would have been more accurate for it to have read "Man of Some Integrity." I have found that I do have integrity. It's there. But I don't have enough. Left on my own, I tend to quietly compromise my thought life, leave important jobs unfinished, or slack off in general. So I need the additional integrity of men who share my vision for purity and growth, who will remind me on a weekly basis what my weaknesses and life goals are, and who will check up on me to see I'm paying attention to both. That means I need accountability, weekly and without exception.

Confessing our sin isn't too hard—how do we deny the obvious? And *making* a commitment to abstain from sin, though important, is a far cry from *keeping* a commitment. Keeping it requires admitting that you will be inclined to break it if no one else knows about it and holds you to it. And that means admitting your need for accountability.

I have already recommended joining a men's group that meets weekly. Whether a Restored Hope Network referral group (see "Suggested Reading and Resources" at the back of this book), or a Promise Keepers group, or a general men's accountability group, be sure it's a group of men who are committed to encouraging each other on a weekly basis to stay on course, and one in which you can be honest about your struggles and goals.

Let your group know, from your first day with them, what specific behavior you're committed to staying away from, and what general goals you're trying to pursue. So if, for example, pornography has been a besetting sin to you, and you're also trying to socialize more and avoid isolation, then you would tell your group about both your struggle and goals and have them ask you each week:

1. Did you use pornography in any form?

2. Did you put yourself in a position where you would have been likely to use it?

3. Did you make some kind of social plans this week?

4. Did you keep them?

5. Have you answered these questions honestly?

It's helpful to actually write these questions out, then give them to your group leader so he knows exactly what to ask you. That keeps your accountability specific and practical. And if you will let other men in on your struggles, I think you'll find it much harder to give in to the pull toward sexual sin when you know that the sin is no longer a private matter. Someone else is involved, and his desire to see you run this race successfully, combined with your own, is a winning combination.

Eight

Attaining and Maintaining Friendship

*Masculinity is an essence that is hard to articulate
but that a boy naturally craves as he craves food
and water. It is something passed between men.*

—FROM *WILD AT HEART* BY JOHN ELDREDGE

The link between a boy's relationship with his father and
his gender identity—his sense of himself as masculine and
his identification with men—cannot be ignored. The
legacy of masculine confidence is either passed to or with-
held from the son, and the results can be seen in the way he
relates to men throughout life.

The studies referred to earlier showed that a pattern of
unsatisfactory father-son relationships often precedes
homosexuality. I'm deliberately using the term "unsatisfactory relationship" rather than "bad father," "rejecting father,"
or similar terms. Too often we place blame on the *individual* rather than the *relationship*, somehow indicting the father
as though he purposefully inflicted pain on his son. In fact,
few fathers knowingly reject or hurt their children, and fewer

still are guilty of deliberate cruelty. In this sense, the problems occurring between father and son may be no one's fault. A father may have been absent out of necessity, leaving the son feeling deliberately abandoned. Or a father may have been psychologically limited, incapable of showing the affection or attention the child needed. A boy may have been born with a sensitive nature, reading rejection or coldness into a father who was, in fact, accepting and available.

Miscommunication, as well, is often the culprit. A father's actions or words can be misread, again creating a misperception in the child's mind. The end result is the same: A boy perceives the father to have a certain attitude toward him, and he responds emotionally to that perception. More often than not, no one is to bless or to blame.

If we must blame anything, it should be the chain of events beginning from infancy which shape a boy's attitude toward father, men, and himself. Those events begin with a son's earliest perceptions of his father, perceptions which the average adult probably can't remember but which had profound effects on his development. A favorable perception of a father's attitude will build confidence in a son. That confidence encourages him to relate freely to his father, male siblings, mentors, or teachers and friends. It's as though an emotional baton is passed between the significant males in a boy's life. With each passage he grows more secure because he gets consistent reassurance from each man he relates to. Without that passage he is crippled to a degree, has less reassurance, and experiences more insecurity.

Interrupting the Chain

Of course, this chain can be interrupted either favorably or unfavorably. A boy can feel unloved by his father, making him hesitant to relate to other men. But another important male might enter his life whose acceptance and interest could undo that hesitancy. That may set his course in a different direction, from insecurity to increased confidence in spite of early problems with his father. Likewise, even a strong foundation in a father's love can be undermined by serious rejection or hostility from other men. The chance of enduring that sort of rejection is better for the boy who has already had a good start with his father. At any rate, the early interactions between father and son lay the groundwork for future male-to-male relations which influence a man's gender identity.

To you, men perhaps seemed distant, unavailable, rejecting. Fear or resentment of them may have been a part of your response to that perception, and that response created an increased need for male love. When that need became sexual, you satisfied it through homosexuality. Then when you realized that homosexual relationships were in conflict with your desire to please God, you gave them up. But you didn't give up the longings for men you had felt for so long. In fact, they have hopefully become stronger than ever.

I say "hopefully" because those longings will motivate you to sustain the kind of relationships that will be a source of healing. Your perception of yourself as a man and of your relations to other men will change as you experience male love in its full, true form.

"Male love" may sound unnatural to some; to other people it might sound downright silly. But if you think about it, it's something all men need and something most men seek—not through romance or sentiment, but through strong bonding and committed friendship.

But male love isn't going to get your address and track you down. You have to put yourself into places and situations where it can be found and experienced. In short, you need to *integrate*.

Over 80 percent of my male clients have expressed dissatisfaction with their social life, especially with other men. Many of them had virtually no social relationships with men, while other clients had some contact with men but felt there was much to be desired in their same-sex friendships. In general, they have felt threatened by men or have tended to idealize certain males to a high degree and cling to them exclusively at the expense of other friendships. Other clients have felt real hostility toward men, getting close to them for a time but then cutting them off early in the friendship. In all cases, pursuing more satisfying relationships with their own sex improved their perception of themselves, induced a different response toward men, and decreased their sexual attractions to them.

Integration, then, is a vital part of growth. And it's no coincidence that better relationships with men accompany less sexual attraction toward them.

Healthy Men

Having confronted your current relationships and corrected the parts needing correction, you move on toward new relationships or new ways to relate, or both. That's what integration is all about. Integration happens when you develop ongoing relationships with healthy men. I don't assume that you have never had a healthy relationship with a man, but I will assume that you haven't had *enough* intimacy with men. Your attraction to sexual encounters with men speaks of a need—one that remains and still looks for satisfaction.

Let's clarify this concept of "healthy men." *Health* is a very subjective term. To a degree, all of us are unhealthy. As long as we're imperfect, a fact I hope you won't dispute, we're unhealthy in some ways. So in that sense there are no perfectly healthy men. But there are men who are generally healthy, men who are secure in their gender identity, who experience normal sexual attractions to women, and who are confident and comfortable with other men. Additionally, they're reasonably stable, living moderate, exemplary lifestyles and making valid contributions to their communities. They are, in other words, men worth emulating and identifying with.

Are they better than you? Hardly. You may already have many of their qualities, even if you don't realize it. And there are probably qualities you have that are lacking in them. So you have much to contribute to them, just as they have a good deal to contribute to you. Integrating with them would be to your mutual benefit.

And yet avoiding healthy men may well be your pattern. This is especially ironic because I believe each man—including you—has the potential to be such a man. In fact, so many men wrestling with homosexuality already are healthy in most ways, yet they don't know it. They don't identify with healthy men, feeling somehow unsettled to enjoy their company.

Often this happens because of the concepts that healthy men represent: male confidence, authority, strength. Those are the very qualities that a father represents to a growing boy. I'm convinced that, just as a man felt alienated from his father early in life, he will likewise feel alienated from those qualities that his father represented *and* from other men who also represent them.

What kind of men have you felt most comfortable with? Your response will be revealing. I don't necessarily mean what kind of men you like and admire the most, but what kind you have felt *comfortable* with. Or, better yet, what kind of men do you feel entitled to socialize with and befriend?

I have found that boys experiencing gender-identity problems cling to other boys who seem nonthreatening or nonmasculine. They seem safe to each other, so they establish friendships based not on respect and admiration but on safety. As one of my counselees put it, "I normally hang out with geeks. The Normies scare me."

"Normies" represent the qualities you may admire and want for yourself, but you may also fear rejection or scorn from the men who have those qualities.

That's why integration with those guys is so vital! Until you experience normal relationships with them, which will include their acceptance of you and extension of friendship to you, you will go on assuming you are not like them, or are less of a man than they are. And as long as that's your perception, you will still respond with longings for love from men who represent all the qualities you felt were unavailable to you. Until you experience healthy male friendship, you will go on longing for sexual love from idealized male figures. One way or another you are going to strive for masculine contact. Why not strive for it from the right source in the right way?

The Continuing Need

I mentioned earlier the need a boy/man has for a nurturer, a mentor, and a comrade, and pointed out the absence of these figures as playing a crucial role in the development of an insecure gender identity. I should point out, though, our *continuing* need for each of these figures. To a degree we always need them, and the need for each should not be taken as a sign of immaturity. Instead, it is the *degree of need* for each which determines our security and general health. Grown men, if they're honest, will admit a need to lean on another man for nurturing during particularly weak and stressful times. A certain amount of mentoring is also needed, as a man passes into different phases of his career and life experiences. And, of course, he will always need the security and challenge that comes with camaraderie.

But our development requires a certain emphasis on each of these. The male infant, for example, craves large doses of nurturing. Much of it will come from his mother, and rightfully so. But if the father is not nurturing the boy as well, he may develop a craving for male nurturing, along with a belief that it's not going to be available to him. That creates the perception, need, and response mentioned earlier: "I want a man's comfort and reassurance, but I can't have it, so there must be something wrong with me."

The young boy likewise needs mentoring, whether from a father or an older figure. Siblings, teachers, coaches, or older friends provide this vital part of development. And comrades are always needed, especially when a child has reached a level of security achieved through his relationship with a nurturing male and a mentor.

A man will crave the kind of relationship he has lacked, whether early in life or throughout life. That craving, far from being unnatural, is a good, healthy striving for the very thing the man needs. And that striving should be identified, respected, and satisfied. Your integration should include nurturing, mentoring, and comradeship, with an emphasis on the kind of relationship you have the strongest desire for.

Nurturing

Male nurturing is a boy's earliest experience of his father's love. Infants are, ideally, accepted unreservedly by their dads. In a healthy family, a father gives his infant son unqualified affection and attention. He delights in his boy, cooing over him and regarding him with admiration. He displays open affection for the child, comforting him, playing with him, and—very important—actively pursuing him. He makes his son feel wanted and sought after, a prize and delight to his father.

If this nurturing was not expressed or perceived by the child, he will go on craving it. If he didn't get it from Dad, he'll look elsewhere. His body may grow, but he will retain the unsatisfied longings for nurturing from a strong father figure, even when he himself is old enough to be a father.

Some people would call this childishness. I call it legitimate hunger. And legitimate hunger can be satisfied at any stage of life. If you crave male nurturing, I suggest that you find it rather than be ashamed of your need for it, because that need isn't going anywhere. It will remain a part of you as long as it remains unsatisfied. Satisfaction, in this case, comes by finding a male nurturer.

Nurturers aren't hard to find. They're pastors, therapists, ministry leaders—any kind of man who dedicates himself, professionally or privately, to the welfare of other men. He's easy to spot: He extends himself, whether by presenting himself specifically as someone who is available to help other people or else by his interactions with other men. There is a strength about him, tempered with warmth, which draws other people to him. He is known, at least implicitly, as a father figure. He is someone you can look up to and lean on.

The key element of your relationship with him is *safety*. A Nurturer is there to provide a safe place to expose your conflicts, to be honest about your feelings without fear of retaliation or rebuke. He is perhaps the one person you can let your guard down with, the one who is available to listen to all your frustrations without making you feel stupid for having them. In fact, in his presence you feel highly valued no matter what you're going through. He expresses consistent goodwill to you, encouraging you without being patronizing, offering sympathy without degrading you. He believes in you. Knowing that gives you a special kind of encouragement.

Obviously your bond with a Nurturer is like a re-creation of the father/son relationship. Some might say it's like having the father you never had; I say just the opposite. Relating to a Nurturer means, sooner or later, experiencing some of the unfinished business between you and your natural father. That signals the therapeutic experience called *transference*—one that is common between counselor and counselee but can also occur between a man and another man who becomes a significant father figure to him.

Transference means the transferring of strong perceptions, responses, and unresolved conflicts between you and someone from the past onto someone in the present. It's a psycho-analytical term describing the patient's response to the analyst when the patient may view the analyst the way he viewed his father (or other important figures from his early years). He may assume that the analyst feels toward him the way his father did, and will respond accordingly. So a patient who always felt demeaned by his father will eventually feel that his analyst is also demeaning him. He will read contempt into the analyst's facial expressions or interpret his remarks as being sarcastic or overly critical. I see this phenomenon happen in both professional and nonprofessional relationships.

That's the value of a nurturing relationship. Not only does it give you a chance to experience acceptance and comfort from a caring man, but it also lets you reexperience early conflicts, identify them, and discuss them openly. I have come to see this as a turning point in my own clients' progress. Much of the early counseling phase is pleasant enough, because the counselee is learning about himself and enjoying the safety and empathy that our relationship offers. But sooner or later

I disappoint my clients. It's inevitable. Either I err one way or another, or the client begins to perceive me as he used to perceive his own father. Suddenly I'm no longer the Good Counselor but Jack the Ripper, M.A. That used to terrify me; now I see it as an opportunity to work with and grow with the client. And in so doing, our relationship becomes stronger and more productive.

So if you need a Nurturer—a father figure, if you will—find one. But don't expect perfection. You wouldn't really mature if you had it, anyway, because we grow up emotionally when we accept the limitations of people we rely on without rejecting them.

Mentoring

There is a fine line between Nurturers and Mentors. Although a certain amount of teaching may come from a Nurturer, his primary role is to provide comfort, affection, and reassurance. Similarly, a Mentor might provide some nurturing, but his primary role is to provide teaching and encouragement toward certain goals. The emphasis on one or the other is what distinguishes a Nurturer from a Mentor.

In the *McGill Report on Male Intimacy*, Dr. Michael McGill refers to this distinction by saying, "This strange combination of parent and peer seems to be the unique feature of these male mentor relationships. A mentor offers a man the guidance of a parent, the compassion of a peer without the competition."[1]

Mentors fill an important need in developing boys. They are still, of course, looking up to men or older boys in general. But they're also becoming independent enough to need less of their father's unconditional nurturing. They look for other men to emulate, men they can admire and identify with. Of course, they may admire and identify with their father, but they also need to spread out and test their abilities to relate to other admired male figures.

Other cultures are smarter than ours in this respect. Some tribal communities, for example, make a definite ritual out of same-sex identification and bonding. When their young men reach puberty, the other men take them out and initiate them, through various rites, into masculine society. Boys know they're accepted by older men, making the transition from boyhood to adolescence one of honor and security.

A Mentor, then, is a male who functions as a teacher and a guide. In childhood an older brother often serves as a mentor. Men outside the family, as well, fill the mentoring role. That's why there's a double value to boyhood experiences like music lessons, schooling, and athletics. They expose a boy to male figures who fine-tune his abilities while increasing his confidence with men in general. As a child is made secure through the acceptance and reassurance he gets from the Nurturer, he can move on to the mentoring relationship, which is a bit more demanding. There again the fine line is drawn between Mentorer and Nurturer: A Mentor is a male that a boy wants to emulate and learn from, not just bond with.

When you find someone with experience and proficiency in a part of life you would like to improve in, and when that person is willing to help guide you into more expertise in that area, you've found a Mentor. That part of life may be a specific skill, or it may be a way of expression. (Some men, for instance, look for Mentors to help them develop more masculine ways of expressing themselves.) Like nurturing, mentoring is a valuable experience which satisfies a legitimate need.

In the legend of the Knights of the Round Table, a young knave called Percival was fascinated by the knight Sir Lancelot. Lancelot represented so much of what Percival wanted to have: bravery, competence, honor. So Percival sought him out as a Mentor. He chased Lancelot, literally, until he convinced him to take him on as an apprentice. Through Lancelot, Percival learned the skills of knighthood and eventually was inducted into the company of the Round Table. Percival had the desire and potential to become a knight; Lancelot's willingness to mentor him bridged the gap between his desire and his knighthood. This legendary form of mentoring is worked out in hundreds of ways in modern life.

That's what Mentors are for. If there's an area of life you want to excel in, find someone who already excels in it and ask for help. The technical benefit of this will be your increased ability in a certain area. The long-term benefit will be an increased confidence in your masculinity and a deepened security in your gender identity. Remember, gender identity is your sense of yourself as being masculine, and masculinity is enhanced each time you conquer an old fear and adopt a new form of behavior.

Comrades

A Comrade is a companion, the kind of friend usually described as a "buddy," with whom you have an ongoing, intimate bond. It is a relationship based on commonality— common goals, common ideals and principles, and a common interest in investing time and energy into a friendship. The ability to make and maintain such a friendship comes again from a certain amount of confidence. As a boy becomes less dependent on his father's nurturing and gains more confidence by learning from his Mentor, he can establish relationships with equals or peers. With his peers he learns to compete, to be challenged, to find common ground, and to bond. This bonding with peers will have begun in childhood hopefully, but in adolescence it becomes especially important.

The adolescent has become less emotionally dependent on his parents and places more importance on his peer relationships. That's probably why adolescence is a time of such struggle between parents and teenagers. The parents lose some (or a lot) of their clout, and the approval of peers means more to the teenager than his parents' approval does. Conformity marks adolescence. Dressing, talking, and acting like "the other guys" becomes vital to the teenager, and often the bizarre ways that teenagers express themselves are just statements of independence from their parents. Peer relations, or relations with Comrades, are as vital to a healthy gender identity as nurturing and mentoring.

But if nurturing and mentoring haven't occurred, the adolescent boy is ill-equipped to deal with the challenge of peer relationships. That can turn the teenage years into a nightmare of self-doubt and rejection. In fact, many men I have worked with point to their adolescence as a high point of misery in their lives. Lacking the assurance of a solid father/son relationship, they shy away from other boys as well. And other boys certainly don't encourage them to do any differently. Kids are all too often cruel. They sniff out insecurity in a boy and crucify him for it, only encouraging him to avoid efforts at integration with his own kind. That solidifies the boy's long-held perception that he is indeed an outcast, unacceptable to other boys and men in general.

That, combined with our culture's lack of emphasis on male relationships, creates real problems for all of us. All men need other men. We need male friendships that are solid and lasting, yet over and over again we ignore this need or even deny its existence! Strange but true, the American male is often a friendless creature who could learn a lot from his female counterpart. In this area women have us beat, because they seem more aware of their need for each other and are more willing to express it. "In our society," says Elliot Engel, "it seems as if you've got to have a bosom to be a buddy." How sad for all of us.

How sad for you especially, though. If most men have an unsatisfied need for camaraderie, your need for it is doubly strong. If homosexuality is a sexualized emotional need for intimacy, then its resolution can only come when you are getting, without sex, the male intimacy you've been looking for. The answer is not to stop looking, but to look harder.

Finding a Comrade

Looking means using a little common sense and an understanding of the way men bond in our culture. Man-to-man relationships usually depend on an indirect activity— sports, for example—to keep them going. Seldom do men admit to each other the need they have for each other, covering it up with phrases like "Let's play golf" instead of "Let's get together—we need to build our friendship." (Did you notice how funny that sounded? Even I winced a little as I wrote it. That says a lot about our attitude toward male bonding.)

If this is a problem for men in general, it's especially a problem for *you*. Since men—even healthy ones—aren't prone to extend open invitations to bonding, it makes it that much more difficult for you to determine how to get close to the men you need. You can't just walk up to a fellow and say, "Hey, you represent all the qualities of masculinity I've had a sexualized need to merge with. Wanna bond?"

You can't just request time and friendship from other men. But you can, indirectly at first, become a part of their lives by joining them when they're together. That is the safest and most effective way I know to begin integrating—through male group activities.

The problem with this is that male group activities often bring to mind some of the most unnerving moments of childhood and adolescence. Those were times boys bonded through sports, for example—something many of us were terrified of. So to integrate with men in groups, you've got to get past your fear of group activities. More specifically, you have to overcome the fear that you will again be humiliated when you try to "play with the guys."

Of course, "playing with the guys" need not mean sports activities. It can include any kind of group activity that men are participating in. Your job is to find one that is compatible with you. Comrades are found among men, and your relationship with one is built when you have given yourself a chance to meet men, make acquaintances, let the acquaintances evolve into friendships, and let the friends become comrades.

You do this by putting yourself in situations where this can happen (a hard first step, but a necessary one). Then you look for men within the group who seem friendly and receptive to you. That's not too hard; just keep your eyes open and, as Solomon said, show yourself to be friendly. When the door to conversation seems open, pursue it. If you're shy, you may experience a thousand anxieties at this point. But keep in mind the fact that nobody can see those anxieties but you, so don't let them stop you. As you gradually gain acceptance and sense a desire on another man's part to know you better, follow through.

You might feel awfully strange doing this. It can be reminiscent of "cruising," putting the "make" on another man in a sexual sense. Yet there is such a thing as healthy, nonsexual pursuit. Don't back off from it. It's the very thing you need.

The Challenge of Integration

Integration is a challenge, one you will have to accept if you're going to make progress. Only through relationships do we grow; without them we stagnate. Begin by deciding what kind of man-to-man relationship you're needing the most—nurturing, mentoring, camaraderie, or all three. Then make a commitment to aggressively pursue what you need and the kind of man you need it from.

Yes, pursue. I can almost hear someone snickering. "This sounds like some sort of husband-hunting manual!" Not quite, because it's nonsexual, nonromantic love you're looking for. But if you aren't willing to actively look for it, there's no reason to assume you will ever have it. And if you never have it, you'll never get past the need for it. So go for it; you don't really have a choice.

You may balk at this idea. You may retain a childish wish that someone will come along and, seeing how much you need male bonding, offer himself like some kind of nurturing White Knight and say, "Hey, little boy, I'll give you a hand." Don't count on it. No one can see your needs, and most people will never assume you have them. It's up to *you* to create an environment for yourself that will allow relationships to build and grow.

If all of this sounds like nothing more than a "how to make friends and influence people" speech, remember the ultimate goal of integration: to change the early perceptions of yourself that created sexual responses to men in the first place. I am convinced that those perceptions will change only by getting a new, healthy response from other people, and this response will come only when you integrate with them.

That's how it all started. You perceived a response, and your perception shaped your gender identity. To change your perception, you need accepting, positive responses from the kind of men you value and admire. As they favorably respond to you, you begin to see yourself differently. Your confidence grows, your identification with healthy men becomes more solid, and your need for male love begins to be satisfied. And that's when healing occurs—when the needs you have tried to meet indirectly through sex are being met directly through nonsexual intimacy.

Afterthoughts on
Attaining and Maintaining Friendship

In June of 1988, I had my first exposure to theories on father/son bonding, its impact on homosexuality, and the power of healthy male bonding as a healing force.

I was listening to a lecture by psychologist Elizabeth Moberly and her observations matched my own experience and that of the men I had been working with to the letter. This was the answer, I was sure: Homosexuality springs from unmet desires for same-sex bonding with the father and are resolved through same-sex bonding in healthy, godly friendship.

I saw this pattern repeatedly in the men I worked with, especially in the early part of counseling when we would explore family background. Try as I might to take each client case by case, avoid imposing my own theories on them, and let them speak for themselves, whenever we began looking at family dynamics, the father/son problem would show itself. I became convinced that, more than anyone else, men struggling with homosexuality had experienced serious conflicts with Dad.

Then about ten years into my career, my clientele changed. While still counseling homosexual men, I also began seeing heterosexual men addicted to pornography, or who had had adulterous affairs or other sexual and relational problems. And as I began working with heterosexuals (who now make up the majority of my clientele), I was more than a little shocked to see frequently the same father/son conflicts in *their* family history! Even more startling was the realization that they, too, had enormous problems integrating socially and held many of the same fears and misconceptions as my homosexual clients.

Well, well—looks like men in general, not just homosexual ones, have a real problem dealing with each other. And while I stress the need for the homosexual struggler to integrate and follow the principles outlined in this chapter, I now see friendship as a crucial healing component for *any* man involved in sexual sin. So many of us, it seems, have a hunger for friendship without a clue as to how it is built and sustained.

I think men want to be close but haven't been given permission or direction in genuine male bonding. And I think our desire for closeness flows out of our need to be reminded of and connected to our manhood.

After all, the first words uttered about you had nothing to do with your personality, career, or talent. They were all about your sexual identity: "It's a *boy!*"

That was your first identifying factor, ushering in a world of expectations. There would always, from that moment, be a need to fulfill all that was required of a boy. Which meant, of course, there would always be a need to connect with the sources—other boys and men—who could help you meet those requirements.

But traditionally there has been little emphasis on this sort of connection, leaving modern men with a hunger for bonding and a deep uncertainty about its legitimacy. It hasn't been okay to admit our need for each other, even though we have known it's there. How else can you explain the efforts men have been making—sometimes clumsy, often admirable— to reconnect and build each other up?

Take the secular men's movement, popularized by poet Robert Bly in the late 1980s, when thousands of stable, middle-aged American men were going out to "Wild Man" retreats where they would bang drums, weep together, and dance around in loincloths. Of course the rest of us laughed. But they were on to something, and I think we knew it. But many of us—Christian men, in particular—were leery of this approach, so we waited for something more biblical and sensible.

Then came coach Bill McCartney, and the Promise Keepers men's movement. In organizing this hugely successful work, McCartney gave us permission to admit our need for each other's encouragement and accountability, and pushed us toward a deeper commitment to God, family, and each other. Men responded by the millions—relieved, it seems to me, to recognize our interdependence.

Author and lecturer John Eldredge has taken this a notch further with his book *Wild at Heart,* and his seminars by the same title. Drawing largely on Bly's ideas, tempered with his own more Christian perspective, Eldredge has struck a national male chord with his encouragement to foster instead of repress our need for conquest and adventure.

All of which says you are far from alone in your need for male intimacy and in your awkwardness when seeking it out. But I can testify to its worth. The greatest irony I see in my own journey is not my abandonment of homosexuality, because giving up sex with men was not my greatest challenge. Developing closeness with men was. Yet in that closeness, I have come to honestly love the manhood I never thought I had, as I have come to honestly love men.

"It's a boy." That was good news to whomever said it first about you. And good news should be welcomed, repeated, and enjoyed.

Nine

Dating and Marriage

There are three things which are too wonderful for me,
yes, four which I do not understand: the way of an eagle in the
air, the way of a serpent on a rock, the way of a ship in the
midst of the sea, and the way of a man with a virgin.

—PROVERBS 30:18,19

You began this process needing intimacy. Along the way we have discussed nonsexual intimacy, emotional needs which have been sexualized, and the need to discipline yourself to resist sexual immorality, all of which are vital. But your goal has been sexual wholeness, not a nonsexual state. You remain a sexual being, most likely wanting erotic pleasure and committed bonding. That's as it should be. Sex is something Scripture celebrates and should be thoroughly enjoyed. So I hope that as you are dealing with the ways sex has caused serious problems in your life, you haven't developed an anti-sex attitude.

An attitude like that is common to sexual strugglers. Some people try, when resisting sexual sin, to cut themselves off from sexuality altogether. But physical and emotional intimacy with one person is still a primary need for most of us.

I have not yet known a man who, during the growth process, lost his sex drive or desire for committed partnership. Additionally, most of us want a family life. That, too, is a desirable option for the majority.

But marriage is not the Promised Land. It is by no means a cure for sexual problems, nor will it in any way produce heterosexual response. Neither is it proof of a changed sexual orientation. After all, many homosexually oriented people are married. They retain a primary attraction to their own sex, with minimal or no sexual attraction to their spouse. So from the start let's not view marriage as a goal or an indication that anything in particular has been achieved. Anyone can get married.

This needs to be stressed because too many Christians assume they *should* be married, that somehow they're second-rate or incomplete without a partner. And men dealing with homosexuality are prone to view marriage as the ultimate goal which will validate their healing and put a seal on their heterosexuality. But marriage was never meant to be therapy or "proof of a cure."

It goes without saying, too, that marriage is never guaranteed—not to you, not to any single person. A number of factors come into play: meeting the right person, being ready for marital commitment, having the resources to establish a household. So bear in mind that your readiness for a mate is no guarantee you will find one. If you're single, you're in the same position as all singles: You rely, ultimately, on God's sovereign timing.

So let me suggest you do two seemingly contradictory things: Consider marriage a possibility, but don't go out *looking* for a wife. For that matter, don't regard marriage as a goal to be pursued. It may be something you desire, but if you pursue marriage for marriage's sake, you will set yourself up for a premature commitment to the wrong person. Be about the business of living, relating, and working, and your chances of developing a committed relationship will be improved.

If you are living a healthy lifestyle—fellowshiping, working, and socializing with both sexes—you will be interacting with a number of people. Casual friendships with the opposite sex will usually develop, and at some point you might find yourself attracted to one woman in particular. Van Den Aardweg describes the emergence of heterosexual attractions as follows:

> Mostly, the first heterosexual interests come rather unexpectedly, e.g., in the imagination, or upon seeing someone on the street. The first heterosexual infatuations may bear the marks of adolescence, as if the normal psychological growth process is rapidly being replicated. The client... discovers the existence of a sex divergent from his own....The male client eventually feels the enchantment of the female creature, her tender bodily forms and grace stir him erotically....The woman discovers excitement at the idea of being "possessed" and desired by the man.[1]

Of course, heterosexual attractions aren't proof that you've found Miss Right. Attractions are nice to have, exciting if they are relatively new to you, but not enough to base a relationship on. There are more important things to consider before you begin dating someone.

Your mind, as author Josh McDowell puts it, is your most important organ. Before you start a romantic relationship, however casual, consider the qualities of the person you're attracted to, not just the attraction itself. Take your time, converse, and get to know each other. The question should never be, "Am I sexually attracted to this person?" but rather, "Is this a person I admire and would like to know better?"

That goes for anyone, regardless of his background. But it goes doubly for you because, in your eagerness to experience heterosexual love, you may jump into things too quickly. Don't jump the gun on romance; it will come when it's time. Caution and slow progress are the watchwords here.

When attraction and admiration for a person combine, you may want to spend more exclusive, prolonged time together. So go for it—why not? But keep in mind that, if you begin seeing someone regularly, the issue of your past is going to cross your mind. Should the person you're dating know about your struggles with homosexuality? And if so, how early in the relationship should she be told?

While there are no set rules to follow, I strongly feel that the person you are becoming involved with has the right to know about your background early in the relationship. You might make the mistake of keeping it a secret because you're afraid of scaring a potential mate away before she gets to know you better. In my opinion, that's exactly why your partner has a right to know early on. Before she is emotionally invested in you, falling in love and hoping for marriage, she has a right to know what she's getting into and to decide if she wants the relationship to continue.

That may seem unfair to you. After all, what's over is over. But getting to know someone means knowing significant things about that person's background. And like it or not, your homosexuality has played a significant role in your emotional and social history. Far better to be up-front from the start than to be guilty of leading somebody on. And believe me, if you become seriously involved with someone and she discovers your background later in the relationship, she will feel betrayed and possibly mistrustful of you in the future. People don't like secrets, especially when they involve someone they are emotionally invested in.

There are also practical reasons for early disclosure. It's possible that your past involvement in homosexuality is known by other people. Would you want to chance your girlfriend hearing about it from someone other than you? And what about any counseling or specialized ministry you are still involved with? Do you plan on keeping that a secret, too? That will mean cover-up and evasion, which are not the ingredients of a healthy relationship.

Besides, when you keep something important from someone you're getting close to, it interferes with your ability to fully enjoy that person. You'll feel the weight of secrecy and no small amount of anxiety. Yes, you may risk rejection by being honest from the start. But compared with the risk of sowing mistrust and disappointment in the long run, it's better to come clean at the beginning—not necessarily on your first or second date, but at least before you let a dating relationship become steady and serious.

Courtship

You know when things are moving beyond casual dating. You start investing regular time in one person, your thoughts are consistently occupied with her, and the two of you take it for granted that you're "an item." You look forward to your time together, you share more about yourselves, you bond. You feel a genuine need to be with this one person who is now the object of your sexual attraction and emotional affections. Now is the time to ask yourself some hard questions.

"Have I found a best friend or a potential wife?" Sadly, many men find a woman they relate to so well, enjoy so much, and have such fun with that they mistake fondness for romantic interest. Of course, an element of friendship should

exist in any steady relationship. Sometimes that's the only thing keeping it together when attractions and passion fluctuate. But be very honest with yourself—no wishful thinking, no premature declarations of "Straight love, at last!" Is this a romantic friendship, or a friendship masquerading as romance?

If it's a friendship, there's nothing wrong with that. Just don't call it something else. Don't mislead yourself or anyone else. The quest for a normal man/woman bond often leads people to tell themselves they have found it before they really have, and the results can be destructive.

"Is my own life cleaned up enough so that I can shoulder the responsibility of a steady relationship?" A man whose life is out of control has no business being intimately involved with a woman. If you're still sexually active, whether that means occasional backslides or habitual contacts, get your own act cleaned up before taking a courtship any further. Prove to yourself that you can do that much before you presume to handle a serious relationship, because there is no way your activity will not interfere with and damage the person you're involved with.

I'm not saying, mind you, that sexual temptations of any kind disqualify you from dating or courting anyone. To be tempted is no sin; to habitually yield to temptation is proof you've got to get your act together.

"Can I handle someone really knowing me?" You have probably heard it by now—that spooking voice coming from a car you have innocently brushed past: "You're too close to the vehicle. Please step back." Apparently the auto is rigged with a very sensitive device which detects anyone getting "too close." The system warns you, in a none-too-friendly tone, that you've overstepped a certain boundary and there will be trouble if you don't back off.

Obviously this voice alarm is intended to prevent break-ins. But it can't tell what your intentions are when you approach the vehicle. You might just be walking past it with no intention of stopping. You might just be stepping close to admire the make of the car. Or you might simply be getting into your own car which is parked next to it.

But alarms are not exclusively vocal, and they're not limited to autos. We carry them as well. We know when people are getting close—maybe "too close for comfort"—and we react, sometimes sending out unfriendly warning signals without knowing it.

The deepest pain we have felt has been caused by people we've been vulnerable to. We learn early in life that intimacy can be dangerous, that when we enjoy the luxury of closeness, we also take the chance of being wounded by the people we have opened ourselves up to. That teaches most of us to be reasonably cautious, and I suppose that's good. Even Jesus warned us against casting our pearls before swine—that is, we shouldn't give what is precious (including our feelings) to people who will misuse or abuse our gift.

But you may well have experienced more than your share of wounds. By the time you begin a courtship, it may have been years since you have allowed anyone to really know you. And it may have been even longer since you have allowed yourself to truly need another person. When you notice the development of real intimacy, you may start reacting with apprehension and even defensiveness. "Watch it," your alarm system says, "this person is getting too close! Remember what happened last time you let somebody into your heart?"

Besides past hurtful episodes, you may also still be viewing yourself as an essentially unlovable person. Years of being on the "outside" of a rejecting, hostile society may have taught you that you are unusually defective, that if someone really sees inside you, she will abandon you. You don't want that, so you protect yourself against too much closeness, too much self-disclosure. Feeling threatened by imminent rejection, you periodically withdraw.

The other party, though, hasn't the slightest idea what is going on. All she knows is that you are suddenly closed, quiet, moody. She wonders what she's done wrong—something she said, perhaps? And so begins the age-old dialogue between the people afraid of intimacy and the people who want intimacy with them:

> "You're very quiet tonight. Is something wrong?"
>
> "Nothing. Everything's fine." (Translation: "We're getting awfully close here. I think you're starting to pick up on my little oddities and you're about to abandon me, so I'm protecting myself!")
>
> "Your tone of voice doesn't sound all that fine to me. Is it something I've said?"
>
> (Uh-oh, now I've started something.) "No, I'm just a little tired."
>
> "I really think you're keeping something from me. Come on, what is it?"
>
> ("Aha! Rejection's coming any minute now, I can tell. She's probing me. She'll criticize me for being so sensitive. I just know it! Who does she think she is, anyway?")
>
> "No, I said nothing's wrong! I just need some space. Let's call it a night."

You can keep this cycle up indefinitely, or you can choose to openly and honestly talk about your fears. Now is the time to grow up a bit. Admit that closeness is hard for you, that you're afraid of what your partner is going to see as you get to know each other better, and that, irrational as it may be, it makes you want to close yourself off. That's the only way you'll learn that you aren't so freakish, that someone else can know you without damaging you. That alone can bond you and the person you're courting in a relationship that's fuller and safer than ever.

"Is it true love or therapy?" Men in recovery can be a terribly introspective bunch, as can anyone who has gone through therapy or an intense growth process. Like students in their first years of clinical training, they talk incessantly about "issues," "recovery," and the "inner dynamics inherent in every interaction."

Too much "heavy talk" is in some cases just another convenient way of avoiding closeness. Instead of *being* close, some people forever *talk* about intimacy, examining it from every angle but never experiencing it. Common, too, is the tendency of people who have dealt with important personal matters to talk only about "The Really Big Issues of Life." When conversing, they seem to be saying, "Let's play doctor." The result is pop therapy instead of an enjoyable, satisfying courtship.

You know you're playing doctor when you can't watch a movie together without psychoanalyzing the leading man. Or when you're more inclined to "explore the issues" in your relationship than to enjoy it. Or when you can't neck without discussing the rationale behind touch therapy.

I'm leery of anyone who throws out too much jargon, whether it's religious or psychological. The Christian who is forever saying, "Praise the Lord" and punctuates every sentence with "brother" or "sister" sounds a bit phony to me. I usually assume he's trying too hard to convince me he's spiritual. Likewise, the person who is forever analyzing people and things may himself be hiding behind the Doctor Role. I usually feel like asking, "What don't you want me to know about you?"

Ask yourself if you're getting too analytical, too heavy, too serious. Courtship, after all, isn't therapy. And while there's certainly a time to be deep and inward, there's also a time for playfulness, laughter, and even a bit of silliness. See to it that these, too, are a part of your relationship.

The Marriage Question

Eventually, if you're seriously involved, you'll consider marriage. Aside from all the important matters to weigh before you make this decision, let me offer two more questions you should pose to yourself.

"Have I really left home?" Both the Old and New Testament stress the importance of growing up and "leaving home" before marrying. The phrase "therefore shall a man leave his father and mother and cleave to his wife" does not imply any disrespect to the parents. It only means the wife or husband you choose must now become the priority in your life above all other people.

Before going any further, determine whether or not the bonds between you and your parents are healthy. To be ready to leave home, a person not only has to be reasonably independent of parental influences. He or she also needs to have resolved any unfinished business with parents.

Unfinished business—conflicts in your family that have never been resolved or even addressed—will carry over into your marriage. They will affect your ability to fulfill the role of a spouse, and will eventually damage your spouse's relationship with both you and your parents. So before entering into a new family life, be sure your existing one is, as much as possible, free of long-held bitterness or misunderstandings.

"Have I proven my ability to be sexually responsible by maintaining sexual integrity for a significant period of time?" You have been striving to maintain sexual integrity. Have you been successful? Is your private life the sort that would stand up to public scrutiny? If you have been unable thus far to abstain

from sexual immorality, there is no reason to believe that marriage will in any way solve the problem. It will, in fact, add to it. Not only will your sex life remain out of control, but another innocent party will be brought into your immorality and—count on it—your spouse will be damaged by it.

So if you haven't proven to yourself that you are in control of your behavior, delay marriage. Don't even think of taking on the responsibility of managing a household until you have shown you can handle the responsibility of managing yourself.

Part of that responsibility will mean taking precautions. Specifically, if you haven't been tested for the AIDS virus and you have been sexually active during your adult life, get tested—more than once, preferably. There's no excuse for entering into marriage with any doubts about your health or with the possibility of endangering your loved ones. No matter how anxiety-provoking the thought may be to you, you have to resolve this before you consummate your marriage. To do otherwise is immoral and reckless.

Sexual Bonding—Preparing and Enjoying

When you consider the importance of the sexual relationship between wife and husband, it makes no sense not to plan for it. This intimate privilege that distinguishes the transition from courtship to marriage deserves more time, discussion, and preparation than any aspect of the wedding ceremony because it will continue to be a part of your life long after the reception is over and the musicians have been paid.

Couples usually approach their wedding night with nervous anticipation and concerns. For men, the desire to sexually bond is often accompanied by performance anxiety. This may be the first time the groom has had intercourse with a woman. He worries about his ability to perform, to give to

Desires in Conflict

his bride pleasure, to block out past sexual experiences and thoroughly enjoy his wedding night. The bride may have had very unsatisfactory sexual relationships with men in the past. Will it be any better this time? What's expected of her? Will she be treated with respect and gentleness?

Talking diffuses these fears and relieves the anxiety these questions bring up. At this point you should be openly discussing whatever qualms or questions you have about your wedding night. If you have insecurities, talk them out together. If there are specific fears you have about the sex act, name them and ask for your partner's feedback and reassurance. That sort of honesty will go far toward maximizing your sexual pleasure.

Keep in mind, too, the fact that your wedding night is not the one and only time you will be sexually involved. You've got the rest of your married life to enjoy each other! So determine from the start that when you come together it will be for mutual enjoyment and closeness, not just intercourse. Your wedding night is a time to make love, to seek maximum pleasure for your partner, and to express yourself in ways you have been unable to up till now. Keep the sexual relationship in that perspective, and you will find it a source of intense fulfillment.

Marriage is not the answer to the struggle for sexual identity. In many ways it opens up more struggles because being a husband requires you to learn daily about your personhood, your weakness, your sexuality. Being a man with a woman redefines the experience of masculinity. It is an ongoing process of individual and mutual discovery, a permanent struggle to fulfill the most responsible role you can take on.

But what a joyous, worthwhile struggle it is!

Afterthoughts on
Dating and Marriage

Renee sometimes comes with me to speaking events or interviews. Because she's attractive and personable, people warm up to her quickly, often remarking on how fortunate I am and how proud I must be.

And usually a single man will draw me aside, wink, and say, "I hope, when I'm *really* healed, God gives me someone as wonderful as her!"

I never know how to respond, because though it's meant as a compliment, the implication is all wrong. The person assumes I'm *really* healed (whatever that means) because I have a lovely wife. But lovely wives can be married to very unhealed, irresponsible jerks, so Renee's attractiveness is no reflection on my growth. Besides, who ever said diminished homosexual attractions are all there is to healing? What about the hundreds of other sins we all struggle with daily?

But "really healed" or not, God undeniably *did* give me someone wonderful…and unexpected. I didn't count on getting married. I had been in love deeply with two different women, and both relationships had ended badly. I didn't want the complication of marriage, and besides, I couldn't imagine any woman wanting to involve herself with a guy whose background was as checkered as mine.

So when I met Renee, I wrote her off as unattainable. In fact, I didn't muster the nerve to ask her for a date until we had known each other several months. Then, after it was clear we were attracted to each other, I knew I had to tell her my story—the uncensored version.

189

Poor Baby. I dumped it all on her after our second date. She listened calmly but wide-eyed, then made what I still consider a classic understatement: "Well, I guess we'd better take our time."

We are still taking our time. Every year I am reminded how much more there is to learn about each other, how many layers are left to uncover, how much richer it can get. And every year I am more convinced that while *marriage* isn't proof of healing, a *good* marriage is a healing experience.

So if it's on your heart to marry, that is a good thing, provided you get your priorities straight. Look for character, compatibility, and chemistry, in that order.

Character first. Make sure the woman you are involved with is not just a Christian (that should be a no-brainer), but that she is also a woman of character. Look for maturity, honesty, fairness—things only time can reveal (which is yet another reason for long courtships, which I avidly believe in).

Then compatibility. After all, a woman may be godly and of good character, but that doesn't mean you would enjoy going home to her every night. Look for mutual interests, common tastes, and your general comfort level with her. I knew Renee was right for me when I realized it was easy to be with her for extended periods of time without getting bored or restless. We could slip into each other's company without too much effort, which is always a sign of compatibility.

Then chemistry. Usually (to their detriment) couples base a relationship on chemistry first, before looking at compatibility or character. And chemistry is usually easier to detect right off the bat, making it all the easier to assume good chemistry means a good choice. Which is wrong, of course. But good chemistry—that is, mutual sexual attraction—is still essential if you're considering marriage. Part of the marital covenant is the fulfilling of each partner's sexual needs. If there is no sexual attraction, there's no point in pursuing marriage which is, among other things, a sexual contract.

It's appalling to see a man marry a woman he feels no attraction to, hoping by faith to someday want her sexually. Invariably that's a setup for terrible hurt and disappointment. If you have found a woman you love and enjoy, but for whom you feel no attraction, then you've found a good friend, but not a potential spouse. Please, for your sake and hers, do not confuse the two.

I don't like "happily-ever-after" testimonies. They don't ring true because life never works out so neatly. Good marriages aren't birthed by miracles. If they're good, they get that way through hard work, compromise, and surviving tough times together—sometimes happily, sometimes not. And there is always room for growth and improvement in the best of unions. So I don't appreciate someone holding his marriage out as the ideal, as I'm leery of anyone who thinks so highly of himself.

But I don't mind thinking highly of my wife or of the God who brought her into my life when I was so certain it was a life I was going to finish alone. I don't mind hoping you will find the same caliber of woman I did.

And I don't mind hoping that, when you find her, you will have the good sense to know she is worth fighting for, and that you will dare to believe you have been given all that is necessary to win that fight.

Ten

Final Thoughts

Therefore take up the whole armor of God,
that you may be able to withstand in the evil day,
and having done all, to stand.

—Ephesians 6:13

Your struggle for sexual identity will be answered not by becoming sexually perfected, but by becoming sexually mature. And a mature sexual identity is born of a mature self-perception.

You are not simply a homosexual, heterosexual, ex-gay, or whatever. You are a child of God, bearing His image and indwelt by His Spirit. You have imperfections in all aspects of life, but they do not define you, nor do they rule you. If they exist, they exist as minor nuisances, not major bondages. So let's look for a moment at where this journey out of homosexuality has hopefully brought you so far.

Your sexual identity has been clarified as you have begun to understand what factors combined to make up your sexual history, your struggles, your needs. In understanding these factors you have lost the confusion you held for so long about why you retained erotic desires you never asked for or chose.

Along with that understanding came a healthy sense of absolution. You no longer held yourself in contempt for having homosexual desires, although you assumed full responsibility for what you had done with them.

And with that understanding came acceptance. Acceptance is not approval, but a calm realization that there are parts of life you cannot change, including your past, your wounds, your present struggles. You work on them, to be sure, because your identity as a child of God gives you a hunger for freedom from any sort of bondage. But you don't worry about them. They have lost their control over you, including their ability to bring stress and sadness into your life.

With a mature sexual identity comes a commitment to conform your behavior and expression of all kinds, sexual and nonsexual, to God's standards. Having experienced the impact of His Spirit on your sexuality, you want nothing less than the best He has for you. And you have learned that the discipline He requires of you is mandated to ensure that you do indeed experience nothing less than the best. With that knowledge comes assurance and, at long last, peace.

But don't ever say you have arrived. You, like all of us, will continue to struggle against any number of temptations and tendencies as long as you're alive and kicking. Even if you became completely free of any homosexual tendencies, there is a myriad of other issues to deal with. Nothing but your death or the coming of Christ will change that.

Besides, you have no guarantee that you're immune to homosexual struggles. If they are gone, wonderful. But who is to say they'll never return? Don't get too confident—that's always a sign of danger. Maintain your integrity as though it's always in danger of being compromised because, in fact, it is. Remember Paul's warning: "Let him who thinks he stands take heed lest he fall" (1 Corinthians 10:12).

Be careful, too, not to jump into the world of ministry or testimony. Too many men have mistakenly assumed a call to "ex-gay ministry" just because of the process they have gone through. That's a mistake. Your calling in life may have nothing to do with homosexuality and healing. So don't limit your future options because of your past. If you're called to that sort of work, you'll know it. If you feel no special inclination toward it, then let the dead past remain dead.

To that end, let me offer a few closing thoughts on staying on course.

Stay Real

Recognize that sexual temptation is unavoidable in our sex-obsessed culture. Erotic images on billboards, films, television, and through a thousand other stimulants are bombarding you daily. Being a Christian doesn't exempt you from temptation—the godliest of men can fall prey to it. So the first step toward maintaining sexual integrity is to get real. Admit to yourself that sexual temptation is a problem that *you* have to reckon with. Remember John's warning: "If we say that we have no sin, we deceive ourselves" (1 John 1:8).

Stay Serious

You should know by now that sexual sin ravages everyone connected with it. What you may not know is that every sexual fantasy you entertain, every flirtatious conversation you keep up, or every "second look" you indulge in is the seed for AIDS, adultery, a broken heart, a shattered life. Get serious. If you're entertaining lust, you're dancing on a cliff. Take concrete action now while you can. "When desire has conceived, it gives birth to sin; and sin...brings forth death" (James 1:15).

Stay Ready

If you really believe an earthquake is coming someday, you prepare for it by developing an emergency plan. If you really believe sexual temptation is both common and can become lethal, you will make an emergency plan for it, too. Decide in advance what to do when you are tempted: how to distract yourself, whom to call, how to escape close calls. Even the apostle Paul admitted, "Like an athlete I train my body to do what it should, not what it wants to do. Otherwise, I fear that I myself might be declared unfit" (from 1 Corinthians 9:27).

Can you really afford to do less?

Stay Accountable

Sexual sin thrives in the dark. If you are caught up in any sexual vice, one thing is certain: The secrecy surrounding your behavior is what strengthens its hold on you. However ashamed you may feel about admitting your problem to another person, the reality is this: You can't overcome this on your own. If you could, wouldn't you have done so by now? Take a hint from James: "Confess your trespasses to one another, and pray for one another, that you may be healed" (James 5:16). Find a trusted, mature Christian friend to confide in. Make that friend a partner in your recovery, and *never* assume that you have reached a point where you no longer need accountability.

Stay Brutal

I believe there is an eleventh commandment somewhere that says, "Thou Shalt Not Kid Thyself." If you're serious about sexual integrity, you will distance yourself not only from the particular sexual sin you're most prone to (fantasizing, pornography, affairs, prostitution), but you will *also* distance yourself from any person or thing that entices you toward that sin. Sometimes even a legitimate activity (certain movies, music, or clubs, for example) may be okay for other people to indulge in, but not for you. Get brutally honest about your lifestyle. Anything in it that makes you prone to sexual sin has to go. "All things are lawful for me," Paul said, "but all things are not helpful....I will not be brought under the power of any" (1 Corinthians 6:12).

Stay Teachable

Sexual sins are often symptomatic of deeper emotional needs that a man is trying to satisfy in all the wrong ways. Repenting of the sin itself is a necessary first step, but recognizing the conflicts or needs that led you into that behavior may be the next step, requiring some specialized care from a Christian professional. Don't hesitate to seek godly counsel if you're trapped in cycles of ongoing, out-of-control behavior. The answer you need may be more than just "pray and get over it!" King David (who was no stranger to sexual sin, by the way) found refuge in Samuel's wise mentoring (1 Samuel 19:18). If you're willing to seek professional help for taxes, medical care, or career counseling, surely you will be willing to do the same to maintain your sexual integrity.

Stay Comfortable

The problem of sexual temptation isn't going anywhere. It's been with us since time immemorial, and no doubt it will plague us until Christ comes. So get comfortable with the idea that you'll need to manage your sexual desires throughout life, always remembering that your sexual integrity is but a part of the general lifelong sanctification process all Christians go through.

"I count myself not to have attained perfection," Paul told the Philippians. "I am still not all I should be" (from Philippians 3:12,13). So learn to love the *process* of pressing on, not perfection.

Stay Connected

"I've been looking for love in all the wrong places," an old song laments. The sexual sin you are drawn toward may indeed be a cheap (though intense) substitute for love. You can repent of the sin, but not of the need the sin represents. So get love in your life: friendships, family, spouse, fellow believers. A man who truly loves and knows he is truly loved is far less likely to search for what he already has in places he'll never find it. "Why do you spend money for what is not bread, and your wages for what does not satisfy?" Isaiah asked (Isaiah 55:2). Learn to be intimate and authentic. It's one of the best ways to protect your heart and your integrity.

Stay in God's Grace

It isn't the sinless man who makes it to the end; rather, it's the man who has learned to pick himself up after he stumbles. If your struggle seems relentless, remember this: When you commit yourself to sexual integrity, you commit yourself to a *direction*, not to *perfection*. You may stumble along the way. That's no justification for sin, just a realistic view of life in this fallen world. What determines the success or failure of an imperfect man is his willingness to pick himself up, confess his fault, and continue in the direction he committed himself to. Remember Paul's approach:

"Forgetting those things which are behind...I press toward the mark...of the high calling" (Philippians 3:13,14 KJV).

Stay Hungry

What's your passion? What's your calling? How clear are your goals? And, by the way, do you have any fun? The man who doesn't have a life—a passion, a sense of meaning, an ability to play as hard as he works—is a man with an emptiness tailor-made for sexual sin. Life is about more than keeping yourself sexually pure, as important as purity is. It's about knowing who and why you are, where your priorities lie, and where you're headed. If you don't know that much about yourself, you have some serious thinking to do. Commit yourself to developing your life as a good steward of your gifts and opportunities, and make that the context in which you seek to maintain your sexual integrity. Sexual integrity for its own sake is a good thing; sexual integrity for the sake of a higher calling is better. So by all means turn from your sin. But as you do, turn toward a goal-oriented, passionate, meaningful life. That is repentance in its truest, finest sense.

Above everything else, stay grateful, humble, aware of the Lord your God who brought you out of slippery places and set you on a rock. It was He, not you, who created in your heart a dissatisfaction with homosexuality. He disengaged you from habits and tendencies that were destructive. No matter how hard you have striven to learn, to repent, and to grow, it has been His grace that has enabled you to do so. Without it, you would never have made it this far. Glory in the new life you have, by all means. But never forget who gave it to you. Never forget where you are now and where, but for His intervention, you might have been.

Appendix One

The "Born Gay" Question

You hear it repeated so often, it's hard to remember a time when it wasn't the conventional wisdom: "Gay people are born that way." To most, that's an academic issue. To you it's quite a bit more. After all, if you were born homosexual, it might seem unreasonable to expect you to abandon what seems to be an inherited (and therefore immutable) trait. But before accepting the commonly held notion that your sexual desires are genetically determined, let's look at a few of the studies most often touted as "proof" for the "born gay" theory.

In 1991 Dr. LeVay, a neuroscientist at the Salk Institute of La Jolla, California, examined the brains of 41 cadavers: 19 allegedly homosexual men, 16 allegedly heterosexual men, and 6 allegedly heterosexual women. His study focused on a group of neurons in the hypothalamus structure called the interstitial nuclei of the anterior hypothalamus, or the INAH3.

He reported this region of the brain to be larger in heterosexual men than in homosexuals; likewise, he found it to be larger in heterosexual men than in the women he studied. For that reason, he postulated homosexuality to be inborn, the result of size variations in the INAH3, and his findings were published in *Science* in August of 1991.[1] This is the study most often quoted when people insist homosexuality has been "proven" to be inborn. Yet the "inborn" argument based on LeVay's research is *exaggerated* and *misleading* for six reasons.

First, LeVay did not prove homosexuality to be inborn; his results were not uniformly consistent. On the surface it appears *all* of LeVay's homosexual subjects had smaller INAH3s than his heterosexual ones; in fact, three of the homosexual subjects actually had larger INAH3s than the heterosexuals. Additionally, three of the heterosexual subjects had smaller INAH3s than the average homosexual subject. Thus, six of LeVay's 35 male subjects (17 percent of his total study group) contradicted his own theory.[2]

Second, LeVay did not necessarily measure the INAH3 properly. The area LeVay was measuring is quite small—smaller than snowflakes, according to scientists interviewed when his study was released. His peers in the neuroscientific community cannot agree on whether the INAH3 should be measured by its size/volume or by its number of neurons.[3]

Third, it's unclear whether brain structure affects behavior or behavior affects brain structure. Dr. Kenneth Klivington, also of the Salk Institute, points out that neurons can change in response to experience. "You could postulate," he says, "that brain change occurs throughout life, as a consequence of experience."[4] In other words, even if there is a significant difference between the brain structures of heterosexual and homosexual men, it is unclear whether the brain structure caused their homosexuality, or if their homosexuality affected their brain structure.

In fact, one year after LeVay's study was released, Dr. Lewis Baxter of UCLA obtained evidence that behavioral therapy can produce changes in brain circuitry, reinforcing the idea that behavior can and does affect brain structure.[5] Therefore, even if differences *do* exist between the INAH3s of homosexual and heterosexual men, it is possible that the diminished size of the INAH3 of the homosexuals is caused by his behavior, rather than his behavior being caused by the INAH3s size.

Fourth, LeVay was not certain which of his subjects were homosexual and which were heterosexual. Dr. LeVay admits this represents a "distinct shortcoming" in his study. Having only case histories on his subjects to go by (which were by no means guaranteed to provide accurate information about the patient's sexual orientation), he could only assume that, if a patient's records did *not* indicate he was gay, he must have been heterosexual.

Yet 6 of the 16 reportedly heterosexual men studied had died of AIDS, increasing the chances their sexual histories may have been incompletely recorded.[6] If it is uncertain which of LeVay's subjects were heterosexual and which were homosexual, how useful can his conclusions about "differences" between them really be?

Fifth, LeVay did not approach the subject objectively. Dr. LeVay, who is openly homosexual, told *Newsweek* that, after the death of his lover, he was determined to find a genetic cause for homosexuality or he would abandon science altogether. Furthermore, he admitted, he hoped to educate society about homosexuality, affecting legal and religious attitudes toward it.[7] None of which diminishes his credentials as a neuroscientist. But his research can hardly be said to have been unbiased.

Sixth, the scientific community did not by any means unanimously accept Dr. LeVay's study. Comments from other scientists in response to LeVay's work are noteworthy. Dr. Richard Nakamura of the National Institute of Mental Health says it will take a "larger effort to be convinced there is a link between this structure and homosexuality."[8] Dr.

Anne-Fausto Sterling of Brown University is less gentle in her response: "My freshman biology students know enough to sink this study."[9]

Dr. Rochelle Klinger, psychiatrist at Medical College of Virginia, doubts we will "ever find a single cause of homosexuality."[10] And *Scientific American* sums up the reason many professionals approach the INAH3 theory with caution: "LeVay's study has yet to be fully replicated by another researcher."[11]

Another study from the same year (1991) was hailed as proof of homosexuality's inborn nature, when psychologist Michael Bailey of Northwestern University (a gay rights advocate) and psychiatrist Richard Pillard of Boston University School of Medicine (who is openly homosexual) compared sets of identical male twins to fraternal twins (whose genetic ties are less close). In each set, at least one twin was homosexual.

They found that, among the identical twins, 52 percent were both homosexual, as opposed to the fraternal twins, among whom only 22 percent shared a homosexual orientation.[12]

Pillard and Bailey suggested the higher incidence of shared homosexuality among identical twins meant homosexuality was genetic in origin. But this, too, seems misleading.

First, Pillard and Bailey's findings actually indicate that something besides genes must account for homosexuality. If 48 percent of identical twins, who are closely linked genetically, do *not* share the same sexual orientation, then genetics alone *cannot* account for homosexuality. Bailey admitted as much by stating, "There must be something in the environment to yield the discordant twins."[13]

Second, all of the twins Pillard and Bailey studied were raised in the same household. If the sets of twins in which both brothers were homosexual were raised in *separate* homes, it might be easier to believe genes played a role in their sexual development. But since they were all raised in the same households, it's impossible to know what effect environment played and what effect, if any, genes played.

Dr. Fausto-Sterling summarized the problem: "In order for such a study to be at all meaningful, you'd have to look at twins raised apart."[14]

Third, Drs. Pillard and Bailey, like Dr. LeVay, did not approach their subject objectively. Their personal feelings about homosexuality, like Dr. LeVay's, certainly do not disqualify them from doing good research on the subject. But their biases must be, at the very least, considered. Pillard said, in fact, "A genetic component in sexual orientation says, 'This is not a fault,'" and both he and Bailey stated they hoped their work would "disprove homophobic claims."[15]

Fourth, a later study on twins yielded results different from Pillard and Bailey's. In March 1992, the *British Journal of Psychiatry* published a report on homosexuals who are twins (both fraternal and identical) and found that only 20 percent of the homosexual twins had a gay co-twin, leading the researchers to conclude that "genetic factors are insufficient explanation of the development of sexual orientation."[16] Not only, then, has Pillard and Bailey's work not been replicated, but when a similar study was conducted, it had completely different results.

Genetic studies have also attempted to bolster the "born gay" theory. In 1993, Dr. Dean Hamer of the National Cancer Institute studied 40 pairs of nonidentical gay brothers and claimed that 33 of the pairs had inherited the same X-linked genetic markers, thus indicating a genetic cause for homosexuality.[17] And yet, like LeVays' study, Hamer's results have yet to be replicated. Again, it should be noted a lack of replication does *not* mean a study is invalid. It only means the study's conclusions have not been confirmed by further research.

In fact, a later similar study actually contradicted Hamer's conclusions. George Ebers of the University of Western Ontario examined 52 pairs of gay brothers and found "no evidence for a linkage of homosexuality to markers on the X-chromosome or elsewhere."[18]

Ebers also, with an associate, studied 400 families with one or more homosexual males, and found "no evidence for the X-linked, mother-to-son transmission posited by Hamer."[19] Again, like Pillard and Bailey's earlier work, a later study similar to Hamer's yielded clearly different results.

There are more important general points to be made regarding the "born gay" argument. First, *inborn* and *normal* are not necessarily the same. Even if homosexuality is some-day proven to be inborn, *inborn* does not necessarily mean *normal*. Any number of defects or handicaps, for example, may be inborn, but we would hardly call them normal for that reason alone. Why should we be compelled to call homosexuality normal just because it may be inborn?

Second, inborn tendencies toward certain behaviors (like homosexuality) do not make those behaviors moral. Studies in the past 15 years indicate a variety of behaviors may have their roots in genetics or biology. In 1983 the former director of the National Council on Alcoholism reported on a number of chemical events that can produce alcoholism.[20] In 1991, the City of Hope Medical Center found a certain gene present in 77 percent of their alcoholic patients.[21] Obesity and violent behavior are now thought to be genetically influenced.[22] Even infidelity, according to research reported in *Time,* may be in our genes![23]

Surely we're not going to say that obesity, violence, alcoholism, and adultery are legitimate because they were inherited. So it is with homosexuality. Whether inborn or acquired, it is still, like all sexual contact apart from marriage, immoral. And immoral behavior cannot be legitimized by a quick baptism in the gene pool.

Third, we are a fallen race, born in sin. Scripture teaches we inherited a corrupt sin nature affecting us physically and spiritually (Psalm 51:5; Romans 5:12). We were born spiritually dead (John 3:5,6) and physically imperfect (1 Corinthians 15:51-54). We cannot assume that because something is inborn, it is also God-ordained. There are mental, psychological, physical, and sexual aspects of our beings that God never intended us to have. *Inborn,* in short, does not mean "divinely sanctioned."

Born in sin? Certainly. Born with characteristics that could make you prone to many conditions later in life, homosexuality included? Possibly.

But born gay? Questionable. Very, very questionable.

Appendix
Two
Pro-Gay Theology

At some point you will be presented with a new way of looking at the Bible and, in particular, the Bible verses that mention homosexuality. This "new way" will tell you these verses have been misinterpreted, that they do not apply to homosexuality, and that Scripture never really condemns same-sex erotic behavior. I call this "new way" the pro-gay theology.

Pro-gay theology meets every Bible verse referring to homosexuality head-on and attempts to explain why each verse is misunderstood today. It is a bold, rapidly growing revision of the Bible which many Christians find difficult to refute.

That is because these arguments take what is obvious and claim to have discovered a different, heretofore hidden meaning. To illustrate, let us take a fairly straightforward scripture: "Come unto me, all ye that labour and are heavy laden, and I will give you rest" (Matthew 11:28 KJV). The meaning is clear: Jesus invites the weary to come to Him for rest. No need to check the original Greek or review the cultural context—the scripture is clear.

Now suppose someone tells you they have done an extensive word study on this verse and discovered Jesus was really inviting pregnant women to stay at His maternity ward in

Nazareth. It seems ridiculous; the context so clearly points to something else. But if you have not taken the time to study the original Greek in this verse, you cannot technically refute the "maternity ward" idea, though common sense tells you it is nonsense.

That is the power of the pro-gay theology. It takes scriptures we are all familiar with, gives them an entirely new interpretation, backs its claims with well-credentialed scholars, and gives birth to a new sexual ethic. Common sense may reject it, but until this theology is examined a bit more closely, it's difficult to refute.

To approach pro-gay theology, we will review each scripture referring to homosexuality, establish the traditional view of the scripture, name the pro-gay arguments against that view, and offer a response to each.

Creation/Created Intent— Genesis 1:27,28; 2:18,23,24 NIV

> So God created man in his own image, in the image of God he created him; male and female he created them. God blessed them and said to them, "Be fruitful and increase in number; fill the earth and subdue it. Rule over the fish of the sea and the birds of the air and over every living creature that moves on the ground."
>
> The LORD God said, "It is not good for the man to be alone. I will make a helper suitable for him."...The man said, "This is now bone of my bones and flesh of my flesh; she shall be called 'woman,' for she was taken out of man." For this reason a man will leave his father and mother and be united to his wife, and they will become one flesh.

Traditional View

God's intention for human sexual relationships is limited to heterosexual union between a man and a woman in marriage.

Pro-Gay Argument

The Genesis account does not *forbid* homosexuality; it simply does not refer to it, for obvious reasons. A gay couple could hardly begin the population process. But these verses cannot be seen as a model for all couples. Many heterosexual couples are childless or unable to have sexual relations. Are they in sin because they do not conform to the Genesis account?

Response #1

While it is true this passage does not forbid homosexual relations, it does provide the primary model for sexuality by which other forms of sexual expression must be judged. Thomas Schmidt puts it well:

> It [Genesis] provides a basis for Biblical commands and for subsequent reflection on the part of those who wish to construct a sexual ethic to meet changing situations—it is appropriate for us to explore the relevance of Biblical commands about marriage and to evaluate modern homosexuality in light of Genesis.[1]

Stanton Jones, regarding Creation as a model for sexuality, adds, "The heart of Christian morality is this: God made sexual union for a purpose—the uniting of husband and wife into one flesh in marriage. God uses sexual intercourse, full sexual intimacy, to weld two people together."[2]

Response #2

The male-female union, introduced in Genesis, is the only model of sexual behavior consistently praised in both Old and New Testaments. While other forms of behavior (polygamy and the use of concubines, for example) are introduced and even allowed in the Old Testament, a monogamous relationship between husband and wife is the standard upheld as the ideal within Scripture. While the old phrase, "God created Adam and Eve, not Adam and Steve" seems flippant, it is a fair assessment of created intent. Whereas heterosexuality is commended throughout the Bible, not once is a homosexual relationship mentioned in anything but negative terms.

The Destruction of Sodom—Genesis 19:4-9 NIV

> Before they [the angels visiting Lot to judge the wickedness of Sodom and determine whether or not to spare it] had gone to bed, all the men from every part of the city of Sodom—both young and old—surrounded the house. They called to Lot, "Where are the men who came to you tonight? Bring them out to us so that we can have sex with them [lit., 'so we may know them']." Lot went outside to meet them...and said, "No, my friends. Don't do this wicked thing. Look, I have two daughters who have never slept with a man. Let me bring them out to you, and you can do what you like with them. But don't do anything to these men." ...And they said... "We'll treat you worse than them."

Traditional Position

The men of Sodom were attempting homosexual contact with Lot's visitors. Sodom was subsequently destroyed for its great wickedness, homosexuality playing a major role in its destruction.

Pro-Gay Argument #1

Sodom was destroyed because of the inhospitality of its citizens, not because of homosexuality. Professor John Boswell in *Christianity, Social Tolerance and Homosexuality* supports this view, basing it on two assumptions: first, that Lot was violating Sodom's custom by entertaining guests without the permission of the city's elders,[3] thus prompting the demand to bring the men out "so we may know them"; second, that the Hebrew word for "to know," *yada*, did not necessarily have a sexual connotation. The Hebrew word *yada* appears 943 times in the Old Testament. It carries a sexual meaning perhaps 10 of those 943 times. The argument, then, is that the men of Sodom had no sexual intentions toward Lot's visitors.

Response

The argument makes no sense in light of Lot's responses. His first response, "Don't do this wicked thing," could hardly apply to a simple request to "get to know" his guests. His second response is especially telling: he answered their demands by offering his two virgin daughters—another senseless gesture if the men wanted only a social knowledge of his guests. And why, if these men had innocent intentions, was the city destroyed for inhospitality? Whose rudeness was being judged—Lot's, or Sodom's citizens?

The theory raises more questions than it answers. While Boswell and Bailey are correct in pointing out the seriousness of inhospitality in biblical times, inhospitality alone cannot account for the severity of Lot's response to the men or for the judgment that soon followed.

Argument #2 (regarding Sodom)

Sodom was destroyed for attempted rape, not homosexuality. This argument is more common. It is proposed by author Virginia Mollenkott and others, and is far more plausible than the inhospitality theory. "Violence—forcing sexual activity upon another—is the real point of this story," Mollenkott explains.[4] Accordingly, homosexuality had nothing to do with Sodom's destruction. Had the attempted rape been heterosexual in nature, judgment would have fallen just the same. Violence, not homosexuality, was being punished when Sodom fell.

Response

The argument is partially true; the men of Sodom certainly were proposing rape. But for such an event to include "all the men from every part of the city of Sodom—both young and old," homosexuality must have been commonly practiced. Mollenkott makes a persuasive case for the event being much like a prison rape or the kind of assaults conquering armies would commit against vanquished enemies,[5] but her argument is weakened by Professor Thomas Schmidt's cited evidence in early literature connecting Sodom with more general homosexual practices:

> The second-century B.C. Testament of the Twelve Patriarchs labels the Sodomites "sexually promiscuous" (Testimony of Benjamin 9:1) and refers to "Sodom, which departed from the order of nature" (Testament of Nephtali 3:4). From the same time period, Jubilees specifies that the Sodomites were "polluting themselves and fornicating in their flesh" (16:5, compare 20:5-6). Both Philo and Josephus plainly name same-sex relations as the characteristic view of Sodom.[6]

Argument #3 (regarding Sodom)

The real sins of Sodom, according to Ezekiel 16:49 NIV, were that it was "arrogant, overfed and unconcerned; they did not help the poor and needy." These have nothing to do with homosexuality.

Response

Again, the argument is partially true. When Sodom was destroyed, homosexuality was only a part—or symptom—of its wickedness. Romans chapter 1 gives a similar illustration, describing the generally corrupt condition of humanity, while citing homosexuality as a symptom of that corruption. But Ezekiel also says of the Sodomites, "They were haughty and did detestable things before me" (16:50). The sexual nature of these "detestable" things is suggested in 2 Peter 2:6,7 NIV: "If he [God] condemned the cities of Sodom and Gomorrah by burning them to ashes, and made them an example of what is going to happen to the ungodly; and if he rescued Lot, a righteous man, who was distressed by the filthy lives of lawless men..." And again in Jude 7 NIV: "In a similar way, Sodom and Gomorrah and the surrounding towns gave themselves up to sexual immorality and perversion. They serve as an example of those who suffer the punishment of eternal fire."

Dr. Bruce Metzger of Princeton Theological Seminary mentions other references to Sodom's sexual immorality in 3 Maccabees 2:5: "the people of Sodom who acted arrogantly, who were notorious for their vices." And again in Jubilees 16:6: "the uncleanness of the Sodomites."[7]

The pro-gay interpretation of Sodom's destruction has some merit. Homosexual rape was attempted, and the Sodomites were certainly guilty of sins other than homosexuality. But in light of the number of men willing to join in the rape and the many other references, both biblical and extrabiblical, to Sodom's sexual sins, it is likely homosexuality was widely practiced among the Sodomites. It is also likely that the sin for which they are named was one of many reasons judgment finally fell on them.

The Levitical Law—Leviticus 18:22; 20:13 NIV

> Do not lie with a man as one lies with a woman; that is *detestable* [or, "an abomination"— emphasis added].

> If a man lies with a man as one lies with a woman, both of them have done what is *detestable* [or, "an abomination"—emphasis added]. They must be put to death; their blood will be on their own heads.

Traditional Position

Under Levitical law homosexuality was one of many abominable practices punishable by death.

Pro-Gay Argument

The practices mentioned in these chapters of Leviticus have to do with idolatry, not homosexuality. The Hebrew word for "abomination," according to Boswell, has less to do with something intrinsically evil and more to do with ritual uncleanness.[8] The Metropolitan Community Church's pamphlet, "Homosexuality: Not a Sin, Not a Sickness," makes the same point: "The (Hebrew word for abomination) found in Leviticus is usually associated with idolatry."[9]

Gay author Roger Biery agrees, associating the type of homosexuality forbidden in Leviticus with idolatrous practices. Pro-gay authors refer to the heathen rituals of the Canaanites—rituals including both homosexual and heterosexual prostitution—as reasons God prohibited homosexuality among His people. They contend that homosexuality itself was not the problem, but rather association with idolatry and, at times, the way homosexuality was practiced as a part of idol worship. In other words, God was not prohibiting the kind of homosexuality we see today. He forbade the sort which incorporated idolatry.

Response #1 (to Levitical law)

The prohibitions against homosexuality in Leviticus 18 and 20 appear alongside other sexual sins—adultery and incest, for example—which are forbidden in both Old and New Testaments, completely apart from the Levitical codes. Scriptural references to these sexual practices, both before and after Leviticus, show God's displeasure with them, whether or not any ceremony or idolatry is involved.

Response #2 (to Levitical law)

Despite the Metropolitan Community Church's contention that the word for "abomination" *(toevah)* is usually associated with idolatry, it in fact appears in Proverbs 6:16-19 NIV in connection with sins having nothing to do with idolatry or pagan ceremony:

> There are six things the LORD hates, seven that are *detestable* ["an abomination" or *toevah*—emphasis added] to him: haughty eyes, a lying tongue, hands that shed innocent blood, a heart that devises wicked schemes, feet that are quick to rush into evil, a false witness who pours out lies and a man who stirs up dissension among brothers.

Idolatry plays no part in these scriptures; clearly, then, *toevah* is not limited to idolatrous practices.

Response #3 (to Levitical law)

If the practices in Leviticus 18 and 20 are condemned only because of their association with idolatry, then it logically follows they would be permissible if they were committed apart from idolatry. That would mean incest, adultery, bestiality, and child sacrifice (all of which are listed in these chapters) are only condemned when associated with idolatry; otherwise, they are allowable. No serious reader of these passages could accept such a premise.

Christ's Teachings and Homosexuality

This argument is a favorite at gay parades. Invariably, when the "gay Christian" movement is represented, someone in their group will hold up a sign saying, "What Jesus Said About Homosexuality: _____." The idea, of course, is that if Jesus did not specifically forbid a behavior, then the behavior must not have been important to Him. Stretching the point further, this argument assumes that if Jesus was not manifestly concerned about something, we shouldn't be, either.

Troy Perry makes much of this argument based on silence (as most gay Christian leaders do): "As for the question, 'What did Jesus say about homosexuality?' the answer is simple. Jesus said nothing. Not one thing. Nothing! Jesus was more interested in love."[10]

According to the argument of silence, if Jesus did not talk about it, neither should we.

Response:

The argument is misleading and illogical for four reasons. First, the argument assumes the Gospels are more authoritative than the rest of the books in the Bible. The idea of a subject being unimportant just because it was not mentioned by Jesus is foreign to the Gospel writers themselves.

At no point did Matthew, Mark, Luke, or John say their books should be elevated above the Torah or, for that matter, any writings yet to come. In other words, the Gospels—and the teachings they contain—are not more important than the rest of the Bible. *All* Scripture is given by inspiration of God. The same Spirit inspiring the authors of the Gospels also inspired the men who wrote the rest of the Bible.

Second, the argument assumes the Gospels are more comprehensive than they really are. Not only are the Gospels no more authoritative than the rest of Scripture, they are not comprehensive either. That is, they do not provide all we need to know by way of doctrine and practical instruction.

Some of the Bible's most important teaching, in fact, does not appear in the Gospels. The doctrine of man's old and new nature (outlined by Paul in Romans 6); the future of Israel and the mystery of the Gentiles (hinted at by Christ but explained more fully in Romans 9–11); the explanation and management of the spiritual gifts (detailed in 1 Corinthians 12 and 14); the priesthood of Christ (illustrated in Hebrews)—all of these appear after the accounts of Christ's life, death, and resurrection. (And we have not even mentioned the entire Old Testament.) Would anyone say none of these doctrines are important because they were not mentioned by Jesus?

Or, put another way, are we really to believe that Jesus did not care about wife beating or incest just because He said nothing about them? Are not the prohibitions against incest in Leviticus and 1 Corinthians, as well as Paul's admonition to husbands to love their wives, enough to instruct us in these matters without being mentioned in the Gospels? There are any number of evil behaviors that Christ did not mention by name. Surely we don't condone them for that reason alone! Likewise, Jesus' silence on homosexuality in no way negates the very specific prohibitions against it which appear elsewhere in both Old and New Testaments.

Third, this argument is inaccurate in that it presumes to know all of what Jesus said. The Gospels do not profess to be a complete account of Jesus' life or teachings. Whole sections of His early years are omitted. Much of what He did and said remains unknown.

Luke wrote his Gospel so Theophilus would "know the certainty of those things, wherein [he had] been instructed" (Luke 1:4 KJV). John's motives are broader: "These are written, that ye might believe that Jesus is the Christ, the Son of God; and that believing ye might have life through his name" (John 20:31). But none of these authors suggested they were recording all of Christ's words. John, in fact, said that would have been an impossibility: "Jesus did many other things as well. If every one of them were written down, I suppose that even the whole world would not have room for the books that would be written" (John 21:25 NIV).

If that is the case, how can we be certain He said nothing about homosexuality? No one can say. But we know there are other equally important subjects left undiscussed in the Gospels but mentioned in detail in other books of the Bible. Homosexuality, while absent from Matthew, Mark, Luke, or John, is conspicuously present in both testaments and, just as conspicuously, it is forbidden.

Fourth, this argument assumes, because Jesus said nothing specific about homosexuality, that He said nothing about heterosexuality as a standard. Jesus referred in the most specific of terms to God's created intent for human sexuality:

> But at the beginning of creation God "made
> them male and female." "For this reason a man
> will leave his father and mother and be united to

> his wife, and the two will become one flesh." So
> they are no longer two, but one. Therefore what
> God has joined together, let man not separate
> (Mark 10:6-9 NIV).

In this passage, Jesus had been presented with a hypothetical question: Is divorce lawful? Instead of giving a simple yes or no, He referred to Genesis and, more specifically, to *created intent* as the standard by which to judge sexual matters. By repeating the Genesis account, He emphasizes four elements of the created intent for marriage and sexual relating: *Independence* was one—a man was to leave his own home to establish his own family with his wife; a *"one flesh"* sexual union was another; and, of course, *monogamy*. But the first element of created intent Jesus stressed was the complementary factor: It was to be a union of *male* and *female, man* and *wife*.

Homosexuality may not have been mentioned by Jesus—many other sexual variations were not, either. But He could not have spelled out the standard for sexual expression more clearly: male to female, joined as God intended them to be. He cannot be assumed to have approved of anything less.

Paul on "Natural" and "Unnatural"— Romans 1:26,27 NIV

> Because of this, God gave them over to
> shameful lusts. Even their women exchanged
> natural relations for unnatural ones. In the same
> way the men also abandoned natural relations
> with women and were inflamed with lust for one
> another. Men committed indecent acts with other
> men, and received in themselves the due penalty
> for their perversion.

Traditional Position

Paul views homosexuality as a symptom of fallen humanity, describing it as unnatural and unseemly.

Pro-Gay Argument #1

Paul is not describing true homosexuals; rather, he is referring to heterosexuals who, as he says "exchanged natural relations." The real sin here is in changing what is natural to the individual. Boswell takes this argument up when he states:

> The persons Paul condemns are manifestly not homosexual: what he derogates are homosexual acts committed by apparently heterosexual persons. The whole point of Romans 1, in fact, is to stigmatize persons who have rejected their calling, gotten off the true path they were once on.[11]

Mollenkott agrees, saying, "What Paul seems to be emphasizing here is that persons who are heterosexual by nature have not only exchanged the true God for a false one but have also exchanged their ability to relate to the opposite sex by indulging in homosexual behavior that is not natural to them."[12]

In short, Paul in Romans 1 describes heterosexuals who have deliberately committed homosexual acts, thus violating their true nature. Homosexuality, if committed by true homosexuals, is not a sin.

Response

Paul is not speaking nearly so subjectively in this passage. There is nothing in his wording to suggest he even recognized such a thing as a "true" homosexual versus a "false" one. He simply describes homosexual behavior as unnatural, no matter who it is committed by.

His wording, in fact, is unusually specific. When he refers to "men" and "women" in these verses, he chooses the Greek words that most emphasize biology: *arsenes* and *theleias*. Both words are rarely used in the New Testament. When they do appear, they appear in verses meant to emphasize the gender of the subject, as in a *male* child *(arsenes)*. In this context, Paul is very pointedly saying the homosexual behavior committed by these people was unnatural to them as males and females *(arsenes* and *theleias)*. He is not considering any such thing as sexual orientation. He is saying, in other words, that homosexuality is *biologically* unnatural—not just unnatural to *heterosexuals,* but unnatural to *anyone.*

Additionally, the fact that these men were "burning in lust" for each other makes it highly unlikely they were heterosexuals experimenting with homosexuality. Their behavior was born of an intense inner desire. Suggesting, as Boswell and Mollenkott do, that they were heterosexuals indulging in homosexual behavior requires unreasonable mental gymnastics. Also, if verses 26 and 27 condemn homosexual actions committed by people to whom they did *not* come naturally, but do not apply to people to whom those actions *do* come naturally, then does not consistency compel us to also allow the practices mentioned in verses 29 and 30—fornication, backbiting, deceit, etc.—so long as the people who commit them are people to whom they *do* come naturally?

Pro-Gay Argument #2 (regarding Romans 1)
This scripture describes people given over to idolatry, not gay Christians who worship the true God. Perry states:

> The homosexual practices cited in Romans
> 1:24-27 were believed to result from idolatry and
> are associated with some very serious offenses as

noted in Romans 1. Taken in this larger context, it should be obvious that such acts are significantly different than loving, responsible lesbian and gay relationships seen today.[13]

Response

Idolatry certainly plays a major role in the first chapter of Romans. Paul begins his writing by describing humanity's rebellion and decision to worship creation rather than the Creator. The pro-gay theorist seizes on this concept to prove that Paul's condemnation of homosexuality does not apply to *him*—he does not worship idols; he is a Christian.

"But," Schmidt cautions, "Paul is not suggesting that a person worships an idol and decides therefore to engage in same-sex relations. Rather, he is suggesting that the general rebellion created the environment for the specific rebellion. A person need not bow before a golden calf to participate in the general human denial of God or to express that denial through specific behaviors."[14]

A common-sense look at the entire chapter bears this out. Several sins other than homosexuality are mentioned in the same passage: "Fornication, wickedness, covetousness, maliciousness; full of envy, murder, debate, deceit, malignity; whisperers, backbiters, haters of God...disobedient to parents" (verses 29,30 KJV).

Will the interpretation applied to verses 26 and 27 also apply to verses 29 and 30? Any sort of intellectual integrity demands it. If verses 26 and 27 apply to people who commit homosexual acts in connection with idolatry, and thus homosexual acts are not sinful if *not* committed in connection with idolatry, then the same must apply to verses 29 and 30 as well.

Therefore, we must assume that fornication, wickedness, covetousness, maliciousness, etc., are also condemned by Paul *only* because they were committed by people involved in idolatry. They *are* permissible otherwise. This is, of course, ridiculous. Like homosexuality, these sins are not just born of idol worship. They are symptomatic of a fallen state. If we are to say that homosexuality is legitimate so long as it's not a result of idol worship, then we also have to say that these other sins are legitimate as well so long as they, too, are not practiced as a result of idolatry.

Paul and *Arsenokoite*— 1 Corinthians 6:9,10; 1 Timothy 1:9,10 NIV

> Do you not know that the wicked will not inherit the kingdom of God? Do not be deceived: Neither the sexually immoral nor idolaters nor adulterers nor male prostitutes nor *homosexual offenders* [abusers of themselves with mankind] …will inherit the kingdom of God (emphasis added).

> We also know that law is made not for good men but for lawbreakers and rebels…adulterers and *perverts* [them that defile themselves with mankind] (emphasis added).

Traditional Position

"Them that defile themselves with mankind" comes from the Greek word *arsenokoite,* meaning "homosexual." Paul is saying that homosexuality is a vice excluding its practitioners from the kingdom of God.

Pro-Gay Argument

Arsenokoite is a word coined by Paul. It never appeared in Greek literature before he used it in these scriptures. There were, at the time, other words for "homosexual." Had he meant to refer to homosexuality, he would have used one of the words already in existence. Most likely, he was referring to male prostitution, which was common at the time.

Boswell points out, accurately, that the word is peculiar to Paul, suggesting he did not have homosexuality in mind when he used it.[15] Prostitution is Boswell's first choice. If not that, he suggests Paul was condemning general immorality. At any rate, the term, according to this argument, means some sort of immoral man but not a homosexual.

Response

Paul coined 179 terms in the New Testament. The terms do not, because they are original, significantly change the context of the verses they appear in. Nor is it remarkable he would have coined this one, considering he derived it directly from the Greek translation of the Old Testament (the Septuagint): "*meta arsenos ou koimethese koiten gyniakos*" (Leviticus 18:22) and "*hos an koimethe meta arsenos koiten gynaikos*" (Leviticus 20:13).

In other words, when Paul adopted the term *arsenokoite*, he took it directly from the Levitical passages in the Greek translation forbidding homosexual behavior. The meaning, then, could not be clearer. Though the term is unique to Paul, it refers specifically to homosexual behavior.

As for the inference that it applies to male prostitution, a breakdown of the word shows it implies nothing of the sort. *Arsene*, as mentioned earlier, appears few times in the New Testament, always referring to "male." *Koite* appears only twice in the New Testament and means "bed," used in a sexual connotation:

> Let us behave decently, as in the daytime, not in orgies and drunkenness, not in *sexual immorality [koite]* and debauchery (Romans 13:13 NIV, emphasis added).

> Marriage should be honored by all, and the
> marriage *bed [koite]* kept pure, for God will judge
> the adulterer *and* all the sexually immoral
> (Hebrews 13:4 NIV, emphasis added).

The two words combined, as Paul used them, put *male* and *bed* together in a sexual sense. There is no hint of prostitution in the meaning of either of the words combined to make *arsenokoite*.

I remember clearly and with inexpressible regret the day I convinced myself it was acceptable to be both gay and Christian. Not only did I embrace the pro-gay theology, I promoted it as well, serving on the staff of the local Metropolitan Community Church, promoting many of the arguments I've just cited. Although years have passed since I realized my error, I'm reminded daily how easily a man can kid himself into accepting what he *wants* to believe, over and above what he *truly* believes.

In an old song by Simon and Garfunkel titled "The Boxer," the issue is nicely put: "All lies and jest, still a man hears what he wants to hear and disregards the rest." May that never be said of you.

Appendix
Three

Seven Questions
Most Frequently Asked
by Parents

In the film *Steel Magnolias,* a young man approaches his parents with a terrible announcement: "Mom, Dad, I want to tell you I have terminal brain cancer."

Shock, terror.

"Just kidding. I'm fine. But I do want to tell you I'm gay."

Now that's a unique way to come out of the closet! And while an approach like that leaves a bit to be desired, it does express the dilemma families face when confronted with a son's (or daughter's) homosexuality. The offspring realize, in most cases, that news of their sexual preference will create an upheaval in the home and that there will usually be a stunned reaction from the parents.

Author Barbara Johnson knows the situation all too well. In her book *Where Does a Mother Go to Resign?* (Bethany House, 1979), she relates the anguish she felt when she discovered her son's homosexuality: "Flashing in my mind was this wonderful son who was so bubbly and happy—such a joy to have around. Thinking of him entwined with some other male brought heaves of heavy sobbing from deep wounds of agony."

Her personal journey from shock to acceptance and a willingness to release her son to God and his own choices makes for compelling (and often humorous) reading. So right off the bat, if you're a parent reading this out of concern for your son, I suggest you get a copy of Johnson's book. For many people it's been an emotional lifesaver.

Mrs. Johnson makes a good point about reaction—one which is the foundation of her ministry, known as Spatula Ministries. She says that when parents hear about a son or daughter's homosexuality, they need a spatula to scrape them off the ceiling. But coming off the ceiling is just the beginning. When a loved one's orientation is homosexual, families are challenged and stretched.

How a family responds to the issue will have much to do with what the issue really is. Is the homosexually oriented family member comfortable with homosexuality? Does he want help? Has he decided to be openly gay? Is he a Christian? These are all questions that help determine how the issue should be approached.

Let's take a brief look at the most common situations that arise when homosexuality hits home, emphasizing what *not* to do as much as what *should* be done.

"My adult son just told me he's gay. What can I do?"

This question is becoming more and more common. Almost half of the phone calls I receive are from parents wanting to know how they can deal with their adult children. As always, the immediate family crisis hits the roots of deeper family issues.

My advice usually follows these lines: First, ascertain your son's feelings about homosexuality. Is he telling you he accepts it? Is he comfortable with it? Has he decided to identify himself with the gay community, or is he simply convinced that homosexuality is a permanent part of his makeup and that, even though he may not be openly gay, he's sure that he will always be that way? Or is he undecided?

Asking these questions will clarify what it is your child is really saying to you. He may be informing you that he is gay and that's it—he has no intention of changing. Or he may be asking you for help, as in "I think I'm gay and I don't want to be. What can I do?"

If a homosexually oriented son tells you he has accepted his homosexuality, he is probably asking you to accept it as well. And on the one hand, you must. You may never accept it as being normal or desirable; however, you have no choice but to accept the fact that to him his attractions are normal. You cannot change his mind; you cannot change his feelings no matter how much you would like to. Likewise, you cannot give your approval or blessing to it. The best you can do is accept this new announcement which, no doubt, will be your greatest challenge.

If your son is asking you for help, by all means make yourself available to him. Help him find the counseling or ministry that will be suitable for him. Support him for having the integrity to face this challenge—a tough one, at that—and deal with it honestly.

Second, acknowledge the compliment your son has paid you by being honest about himself. I know you're thinking, "Some compliment!" but it is one. By disclosing his feelings to you, he is trusting you with very personal, difficult information. He is really asking if he can be honest with you without fear of retaliation. (Remember, unless you discovered his orientation by accident, he really didn't have to tell you at all.)

Acknowledgment does not imply tacit approval. You can appreciate your son's willingness to be open with you without telling him you approve of what he is being open about.

Then express your own feelings. Few homosexuals, when finally opening up to their family, expect their parents to just shrug the news off without a reaction, so be honest. Tell your son how you feel—hurt, angry, frightened, disillusioned—without accusing him. It's one thing to say, "You make me sick! That's disgusting, and I can't stand the sight of you!" It's something else to say, "I feel shocked. I don't know how to take this. I'm really in pain."

When expressing yourself, don't hedge on your own beliefs. It would be unreasonable for your son to expect you to approve of something just because he approves of it. So there's no reason to deny your beliefs or refrain from saying something such as, "Look, I can never believe that homosexuality is normal. That goes against all my principles." This again is different than the more alienating approach: "Don't you know that it's a perversion and you're gonna burn for it?"

Fourth, listen. Let your son explain to you how he reached this decision or understanding. Some parents are afraid to hear their children's experiences because they feel that if they don't preach and condemn, their willingness to listen might be taken for approval. That's not true. When Jesus approached the Samaritan woman in John's Gospel, He didn't even bring up the subject of her sex life, though He knew she had had several husbands in the past and was now living with a man who wasn't her husband. Yet we would hardly take that to be approval on His part!

Finally, state your own limitations. Many parents are put on the defensive when their grown children insist that their gay lovers be allowed to spend the night in the family's home with them or join the family during holiday gatherings. These are not decisions that you should be coerced into. You have to decide what you are and are not comfortable within your own home. This is not forcing your views on your homosexual son. It's just an insistence that you be allowed to decide these things for yourself. Just as you must respect your son's right to live his life as he sees fit, so too must he respect your right to do the same.

And these steps are just the beginning. You now have to deal with the new information you have been given. Your son is gay. Now what? There are three special temptations parents in your position may fall into—temptations you would do well to avoid.

"Is this my fault?"

No. Don't take responsibility for your son's homosexuality. That may seem hard, even contradictory in light of some theories expressed in this book. But remember that even though family dynamics might have something to do with homosexual development, they are certainly not the sole cause. As mentioned earlier, there are probably several factors that combine to create same-sex attraction. Family dynamics may be one of them, but certainly not all of them. Besides, you can't make another person homosexual any more than you can make another person heterosexual. In short, no, you did not do this. You couldn't have, even if you had tried.

That is not to say that if, while examining your own past, you see things you regret and want to discuss with your son, you shouldn't do so. There is nothing wrong with that. But resist the temptation of blaming yourself for the homosexuality you are now aware of. Take responsibility for what you have done; refuse responsibility for what you could never do.

Which brings to mind the question of parental responsibility in general. Is a child's problem in adulthood an indication of parental failures? No, definitely not. Adam and Eve, Isaac, Jacob, David—any number of biblical characters produced offspring that had problems later in life. It is ultimately our fallen nature, not parental shortcomings, that is the cause of all dysfunction, sin, and perversion. To assume responsibility for an adult child's sin is to assume a certain omnipotence. And clearly, whatever else we may be, parents are not omnipotent.

"Isn't there something I can say that will change his mind?"
A common temptation you will face is the urge to rescue your son. How many fathers and mothers have called me saying they're bringing their son in for counseling because they want him "fixed." But the son may have no desire to be "fixed" and may, in fact, have an entirely different concept of what "fixed" means. To force your good intentions on him will only alienate him in the long run, doing real damage to your relationship with him in the future. If and when he wants help, he will seek it for himself. If he does not want help, all the counseling that money can buy won't accomplish a thing.

Your desire to rescue your son is understandable. You have spent years caring for him, protecting him, being his primary source of comfort and training. It's hard—maybe impossible— to relinquish caretaking instincts just because your son has grown up. But really, you have no choice.

Eventually every Christian parent has to release his children to God, their free choices, and the consequences of their own decisions. That is not to imply that you can ever stop caring, worrying, or grieving. But you can't rescue your children. You can't decide for them. You can't control them. Nor should you try.

"Should we just cut him off then?"
A mistake which can lead to the worst sort of tragedies springs from the urge some parents feel to cut their homosexual son off. "If you want to be gay," they say, "then you can just stay out of my life!"

But why? Did your son stop being your offspring the moment you found out about his sexuality? And more to the point, did you ever have an agreement with him that he would live his life as you see fit or else you would have nothing to do with him? Cutting off your relationship with your flesh and blood is a chilling thing to do—a decision you will have to live with long after you have gotten over the shock of your son's homosexuality.

Your son didn't change when he told you about his homosexuality. That's the same boy you have known all these years. You only know more about him now. The question is, Can you continue to have a relationship with him with this newfound knowledge?

I believe you can. And, as much as possible, you should try. There are times when it is impossible, I know. Sometimes sons will have nothing to do with their families unless the family changes its views on homosexuality. That's an unfair, irrational thing to force on anyone. But if both you and your adult son can be clear on this point—we disagree on homosexuality but love each other and want to continue our relationship—then keep the door open. Shock and disappointment in a child's behavior will never sever the bonds existing between you and that child.

"Can parents do anything to prevent their children from becoming homosexual?"

There's no guarantee that if you follow certain guidelines your children will develop a normal sexual orientation. So in that sense, there's nothing you can do to prevent your child from becoming homosexual. The best way to minimize the possibility, though, is to raise your children exactly the way you should be raising them anyway: in a healthy, loving environment of respect, godliness, and support.

Fathers and sons need special times together, as do mothers and daughters. To neglect this is to open the door to any number of problems, homosexuality included. Likewise, relationships between child and parent of the opposite sex should be affirming, especially as the child is moving into adolescence and young adulthood. A father needs to affirm, not inhibit, his daughter's developing womanhood. She needs to know that her father regards her highly, praises her, and celebrates her. A son should be confident that his mother respects his young manhood, admiring it and approving of it. Again, to neglect these areas will create problems of some sort, sexual or otherwise, and to pay attention to them will minimize the risk of sexual difficulties in the future.

"I'm a single mother. Will my son have special problems by not having a father around?"

There's no reason to assume that he will. Of course, a two-parent home is ideal, but many fine, healthy children are being raised in single-parent homes. Remember, the absence of a father is not necessarily traumatic to a boy. Far more traumatic is the presence of a father who seems disinterested or hostile.

If you're concerned, though, about a lack of male presence in your son's life, do what you can to provide him opportunities to interact with other boys and men. Group organizations are especially handy and good for this purpose. But again, never assume the absence of a father guarantees problems, any more than the presence of a father guarantees emotional health.

"I'm still in such pain over my son's homosexuality! Isn't there anything else I can do?"

Yes. Take care of yourself. You can't change the situation, and you can't change someone else's mind, but you can get the help you need to deal with your own feelings.

Find someone to talk to. It can be a good friend, a counselor, or a pastor, as long as it's someone *whom you trust* and *who is removed enough from the situation to give objective, clear feedback.* You need to talk! If there is a group of parents in your situation who meet together, by all means join them (see the Resources section in the back of this book). But whatever you do, don't keep this to yourself. Find an outlet for your feelings and a listening, sympathetic person to lean on.

Don't stop loving your son, but don't clutch him, either. To let go of our children means to acknowledge our inability to change them, rescue them, "fix" them. They were only ours to train and protect for a season, and now the season is over. You still have your life, and to live it fully is at this point the most effective and reasonable thing to do.

Notes

Chapter 1—You Are Here

1. Corrie ten Boom, *The Hiding Place* (New York: Bantam Books, 1971), p. 203.
2. John White, *Eros Defiled* (Downers Grove, IL: InterVarsity Books, 1977), p. 144.
3. Francis Schaeffer, *True Spirituality* (Wheaton, IL: Tyndale House, 1971), p. 26.
4. Ibid., pp. 27-28.
5. Troy Perry, *Don't Be Afraid Anymore* (New York: St. Martin's Press, 1990), pp. 339-40.
6. Francis Schaeffer, *The Great Evangelical Disaster* (Westchester, NY: Good News Publishers, 1984), p. 137.

Chapter 4—Laying the Foundation

1. Dave Hunt, *The Seduction of Christianity* (Eugene, OR: Harvest House, 1984), p. 209.

Chapter 5—Why Me?

1. John Money, *Venuses, Penuses, and Sexology* (Buffalo, NY: Prometheus Books, 1986), p. 252.
2. John Money, *Perspectives in Human Sexuality* (New York: Behavioral Publications, 1974), p. 67.
3. Masters, Brown, and Kolodny, *Human Sexuality* (Boston: Little, Brown and Co., 1984), pp. 319-20.
4. Dr. John DeCecco, editor of the *Journal of Homosexuality,* quoted in *USA Today,* Mar. 1, 1989, p. 4D.
5. Richard Friedman, *Male Homosexuality* (New Haven, CT: Yale University Press, 1988), pp. 57-73.

6. Ibid., p. 71.

7. Ibid., p. 73.

8. W.D. Fairbain, "A Revised Psychopathology of the Psychoses and Psychoneurosis," from Peter Buckley, ed., *Essential Papers on Object Relations* (New York: New York University Press, 1986), p. 83.

Chapter 6—Defining and Experiencing Change

1. Glenn Wood and John Dietrich, *The AIDS Epidemic: Balancing Compassion and Justice* (Portland, OR: Multnomah Press, 1990), p. 238.

2. Reuben Fine, *Psychoanalytic Theory, Male and Female Homosexuality: Psychological Approaches* (New York: New York Center for Psychoanalytic Training, 1987).

3. Gerard Van Den Aardweg, *On the Origins and Treatment of Homosexuality* (New York: Praeger Publishers, 1986), p. 197.

4. Irving Bieber and Toby Bieber, "Male Homosexuality," *Canadian Journal of Psychiatry*, vol. 24, no. 5, 1979, p. 416.

5. Lawrence Hatterer, *Changing Homosexuality in the Male* (New York: McGraw Hill, 1970), p. 138.

6. Patricia Hannigan, president of the Orange County Chapter of the American Psychological Association, quoted in the *Los Angeles Times*, Apr. 5, 1990, interview in Life section.

7. Christopher Rosk, Ph.D., "Conversion Therapy Revisited," *Journal of Pastoral Care*, Spring 2001, pp. 47-67.

8. Ibid.

9. "Historic Gay Rights Advocate Now Believes Change Is Possible" by Dr. Robert Spitzer, who in 1973 assisted the American Psychiatric Association in normalizing homosexuality. Spitzer startled his colleagues when he studied the issue of "change" and came out publicly supporting the idea that homosexuality is changeable. Quotations are from the NARTH web site: http://www.narth.com/docs/spitzer3.html.

10. Robert Epstein, Ph.D., editor of *Psychology Today*, "Am I Anti-Gay? You Decide," Jan./Feb. 2003.

11. Masters and Johnson, *Homosexuality in Perspective* (Boston: Little Brown and Co., 1979), p. 402.

12. Stanton Jones, "The Loving Opposition," *Christianity Today*, July 19, 1993.

13. Kinsey's statistical data is under fire through a book by J. Reisman and E. Eichel, *Kinsey, Sex, and Fraud* (Lafayette, LA: Huntington

House Publishers, 1991). The authors take serious issue with the population from which Kinsey drew his conclusions about the prevalence of homosexuality.

14. Kinsey, Pomery, and Martin, *Sexual Behavior in the Human Male* (Philadelphia: Saunders Press, 1948), pp. 638-41.
15. Ibid., p. 639.

Chapter 7—Maintaining Sexual Integrity

1. "Sexual fantasy...often depends on a basic judgment made about the self; the self assesses whether it is (adequately) masculine." From Richard Friedman, *Male Homosexuality* (New Haven, CT: Yale University Press, 1988), p. 71.

Chapter 8—Attaining and Maintaining Friendship

1. Michael McGill, *The McGill Report on Male Intimacy* (New York: Harper and Row, 1985), p. 182.

Chapter 9—Dating and Marriage

1. Gerard Van Den Aardweg, *On the Origins and Treatment of Homosexuality* (New York: Praeger Publishers, 1986), p. 248.

Appendix 1—The "Born Gay" Question

1. Simon LeVay, "A Difference in Hypothalamic Structure Between Heterosexual and Homosexual Men," *Science*, Aug. 30, 1991, pp. 1034-37.
2. John Ankerberg, "The Myth That Homosexuality Is Due to Biological or Genetic Causes" (research paper), PO Box 8977, Chattanooga, TN 37411.
3. "Is This Child Gay?" *Newsweek*, Sept. 9, 1991, p. 52.
4. Ibid.
5. *Los Angeles Times*, Sept. 16, 1992, p. 1, as cited in NARTH Newsletter, Dec. 1992, p. 1.
6. "Sexual Disorientation: Faulty Research in the Homosexual Debate," *Family* (a publication of the Family Research Council), Oct. 28, 1992, p. 4.
7. "Is This Child Gay?" p. 52.
8. *Los Angeles Times*, Aug. 30, 1991, section A, p. 1.
9. *Time*, Sept. 9, 1991, vol. 138, no. 10, p. 61.
10. *Newsweek*, Sept. 9, 1991, p. 52.
11. *Chronicles of Higher Education*, Feb. 5, 1992, p. A7.

12. "Gay Genes Revisited: Doubts Arise over Research on the Biology of Homosexuality," *Scientific American,* Nov. 1995, p. 26.

13. Bailey and Pillard, "A Genetic Study of Male Sexual Orientation," *Archives of General Psychiatry,* no. 48, 1991, pp. 1089-96.

14. David Gelman, "Born or Bred?" *Newsweek,* Feb. 24, 1992, p. 46.

15. Ibid.

16. King and McDonald, "Homosexuals Who Are Twins," *The British Journal of Psychiatry,* Mar. 1992, vol. 160, p. 409.

17. Dean Hamer, "A Linkage Between DNA Markers on the X Chromosome and Male Sexual Orientation," *Science,* no. 261, July 16, 1993, pp. 321-27.

18. "Gay Genes Revisited: Doubts Arise over Research on the Biology of Homosexuality," *Scientific American,* Nov. 1995, p. 26.

19. Ibid.

20. Frank Siexas, former director of the National Council on Alcoholism, quoted in the *Boston Globe,* Aug. 8, 1983.

21. Joe Dallas, "Born Gay?" *Christianity Today,* June 22, 1992, p. 22.

22. "Rethinking the Origins of Sin," *Los Angeles Times,* May 15, 1993, section A.

23. Robert Wright, "Our Cheating Hearts," *Time,* Aug. 15, 1994, vol. 144, no. 7, pp. 44-52.

Appendix 2—Pro-Gay Theology

1. Thomas Schmidt, *Straight & Narrow?* (Downers Grove: InterVarsity Press, 1995), p. 41.

2. Stanton Jones, "The Loving Opposition," *Christianity Today,* July 19, 1993.

3. John Boswell, *Christianity, Social Tolerance and Homosexuality* (Chicago: University of Chicago Press, 1980), pp. 93-94.

4. Mollenkott and Scanzoni, *Is the Homosexual My Neighbor?* (San Francisco: Harper Collins, 1978), pp. 57-58.

5. Ibid.

6. Schmidt, *Straight & Narrow?* pp. 88-89.

7. Bruce Metzger, "What Does the Bible Have to Say About Homosexuality?" Presbyterians for Renewal, May 1993, p. 7.

8. Boswell, *Christianity, Social Tolerance and Homosexuality,* p. 100.

9. Troy Perry, *Don't Be Afraid Anymore* (New York: St. Martin's Press, 1990), p. 341.

10. Ibid., p. 40.

11. Boswell, *Christianity, Social Tolerance and Homosexuality,* p. 109.

12. Mollenkott, *Is the Homosexual My Neighbor?* pp. 65-66.
13. Perry, *Don't Be Afraid Anymore*, p. 342.
14. Schmidt, *Straight & Narrow?* pp. 78-79.
15. Boswell, *Christianity, Social Tolerance and Homosexuality*, pp. 344-45.

Suggested Reading
and Resources

For Men Wrestling with Sexual Temptation:
Every Man's Battle by Stephen Arterburn and Fred Stoeker
(Waterbrook Press, 2000).

For Women Struggling with Lesbianism:
*Restoring Sexual Identity: Hope for Women Who Struggle with Same-Sex
Attraction* by Anne Paulk (Harvest House, 2003).

For Parents and Family Members with Homosexual Loved Ones:
Someone I Love Is Gay by Bob Davies and Anita Worthen
(InterVarsity Press, 1996).

To Refute the Pro-Gay Biblical Interpretation:
A Strong Delusion by Joe Dallas (Harvest House, 1996).

To Discuss and Debate Issues Related to Homosexuality:
Homosexuality and the Politics of Truth by Jeffrey Santinover (Baker
Book House, 1996).

Help for Sexual Addiction:
The *Every Man's Battle* five-day seminar for men, conducted monthly
by Joe Dallas. Contact New Life Ministries at 1-800-NEW-
LIFE or at *www.newlife.com*.

**To Contact an Organization in Your Area Offering Ministry to
Homosexuals:**
Restored Hope Network at 1-503-927-0869 or
www.restoredhopenetwork.org

**Help and Support for Parents and Family Members with
Homosexual Loved Ones:**
On the West Coast: Living Stones Ministries—626-963-6683 or
www.livingstonesministry.org

On the East Coast: Parents and Friends (PFOX)—703-360-2225 or
   www.pfox.org

**For National Referrals to Professional Counseling for
Homosexuality:**
National Association for the Research and Treatment of
   Homosexuality—818-789-4440 or *www.narth.com*

Resources from
Joe Dallas

Educational materials by Joe Dallas on homosexuality and related issues are available through Genesis Counseling. For a free catalog of audio/CD tapes and other resources, or to book Joe Dallas for a speaking engagement at your church or a seminar, please contact:

Genesis Counseling
17632 Irvine Blvd. Suite 220
Tustin, CA 92780
(714) 502-1463
www.genesiscounseling.org

Other Fine
Harvest House Books

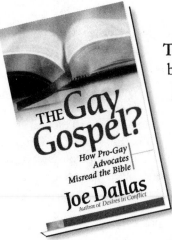

THE GAY GOSPEL?
by *Joe Dallas*

Author and counselor Joe Dallas helps readers understand what pro-gay theology is and how to confront it. In a biblical manner, Dallas examines believers' personal responses and the need for bold love and commitment in their interactions.

This book:

- explains the movement's background and beliefs
- provides a clear, scriptural response to each belief
- shows readers how to extend Christ's love to those living the homosexual lifestyle

This resource is an important one for those who have been unsure how to respond to the growing acceptance of homosexuality in the evangelical community. It offers the balance between conviction and compassion and a practical guide to communicating with those who have embraced the pro-gay Christian movement.

ISBN 978-0-7369-1834-3

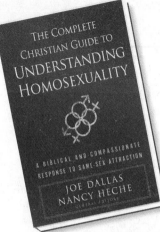

THE COMPLETE CHRISTIAN GUIDE TO UNDERSTANDING HOMOSEXUALITY
by *Joe Dallas* and *Nancy Heche*

One of the hot-button issues of our day is fully addressed in this comprehensive new resource on homosexuality. This well-researched and highly readable guide is the perfect go-to manual for families, church workers, counselors, pastors, civic leaders, schools, and those who themselves struggle with same-sex attraction.

Readers will find the answers to these and many more important questions:

- What is homosexuality?
- Is the tendency for homosexuality genetic?
- How should the church respond?
- What's the proper response when relatives or friends announce they're gay?
- What are the legal and civic ramifications of homosexuality?
- Should homosexuals serve openly in the military?
- What about gay marriage and adoption?

ISBN 978-0-7369-2507-5

RESTORING SEXUAL IDENTITY
by *Anne Paulk*

Restoring Sexual Identity offers answers to the most commonly asked questions from both lesbians desiring change, and friends and relatives of women struggling with same-sex attraction.

- Is lesbianism an inherited predisposition or is it developed in childhood?

- Does becoming a Christian eliminate all desire for members of the same sex?

- What support is available for women who struggle with lesbianism?

- Can a woman be a lesbian and a Christian at the same time?

- How does childhood sexual abuse relate to the development of lesbianism?

These and other important questions are answered as the author draws from her own experience and that of many other former lesbians who participated in an extensive survey on same-sex attraction.

ISBN 978-0-7369-1179-0

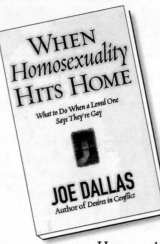

WHEN HOMOSEXUALITY HITS HOME: WHAT TO DO WHEN A LOVED ONE SAYS THEY'RE GAY
by *Joe Dallas*

The heart-wrenching declaration that a loved one is a homosexual is increasingly being heard in Christian households across America. How can this be? What went wrong? Is there a cure?

In this straightforward book, Joe Dallas offers practical counsel, step by step, on how to deal with the many conflicts and emotions parents, grandparents, brothers and sisters, or any other family member will experience when learning of a loved one's homosexuality.

Drawing from his own experience and from his many years of helping families work through this perplexing and unexpected situation, Joe offers scriptural and compassionate advice both to struggling gays and to those who love them.

ISBN 978-0-7369-1201-3